The Modern Bathroom Reader

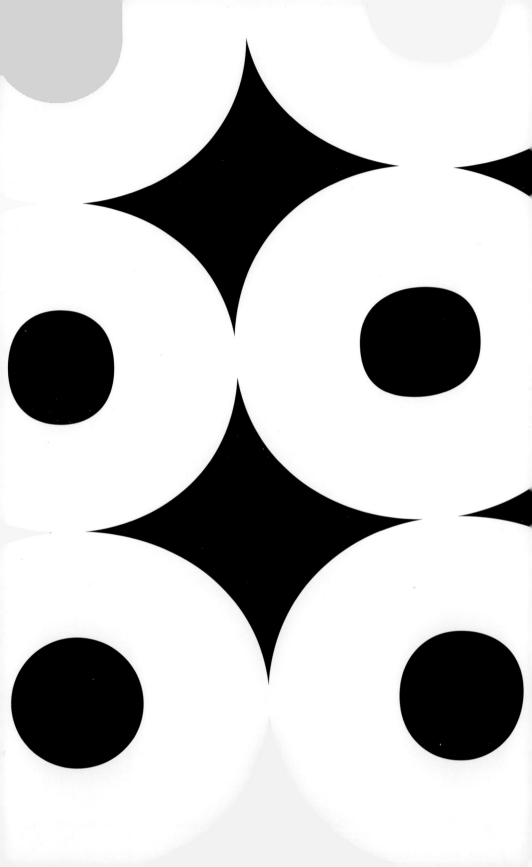

Still not a phone.

The Modern Bathr**oo**m Reader

Fascinating Information for the Perpetually Curious

David Wexter and Emily Williams

Andrews McMeel
PUBLISHING®

To the people who keep asking
"Why?"
no matter how annoying.

Contents

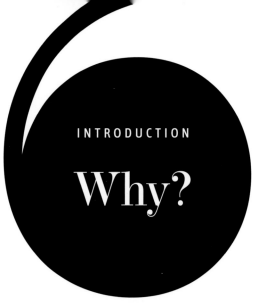

Why?

It's the question that separates the curious from the clueless. It's what keeps us on the edge of our toilet seats, flipping one more page, reading one more line, wondering what the heck weird and wonderful thing we'll read next. It's that feeling of coming alive and chortling to yourself about the weirdness of the world that inspired this book.

Because honestly, when is there time to wonder "Why?" anymore without immediately pulling up Google and finding an answer? Which is great—hey, we're all for questions with answers (why we like trivia so much). But sometimes you don't know the question, or you don't have a question per se, and you just want to feel connected to something bigger than the current screen in front of you. And other times, you're just really, really bored. You've stared at your bathroom wall for long enough, and you'll die of being influenced at if you spend another minute on social media. This book is for those times that try our souls and strain our you-know-whats.

In this book you'll learn about things you didn't know existed, like the neutrino (of which you have three hundred floating around in your pinky finger right now), and things you knew existed but didn't know where they came from, like cheese puffs (which literally puffed into existence by pure accident). You'll be awed by the turnip festival in Oaxaca, the infamous boba tea rivalry in Japan, and the most pristine, pretty mummy you've never heard of in China. You'll be grossed out by the most horrific Jell-O monstrosities known to mankind, and you'll be slightly perturbed (in an adorable way) by vintage slang that just hits different. And to round it all out are the pandas, penguins, parakeets, and other zoological zaniness that make the weird and wacky world go round.

We're not here for those old-school bathroom readers, with their Eurocentric imperialist narratives disguised as "off-color humor." This is not your creepy Uncle J's bathroom reader, where he gets all his worst material for cringe-inducing stories told around the holiday table. This is a bathroom reader for curious and discerning people, for those who don't need or want to dunk on marginalized folks for LOLs. That's why our team of highly literate, scatologically inclined readers have scoured the toilet bowl of the world to bring you only the true, good, fascinating, and *real* stories that are actually worth reading.

So sit back, get comfy in your throne room, drown out the dreary and demanding world, and dive into the surprising and mind-blowing world of *The Modern Bathroom Reader.*

The
Modern
Bathroom
Reader

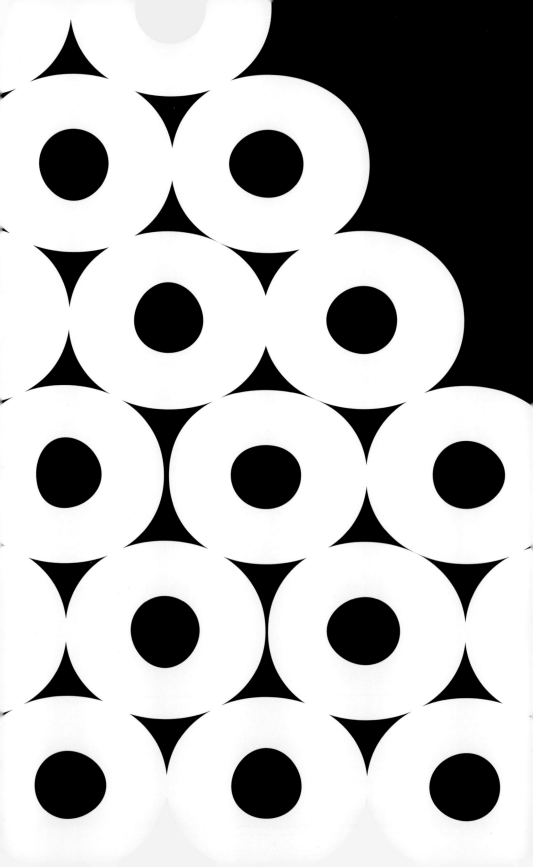

1

Animal Antics to Astound Zoo

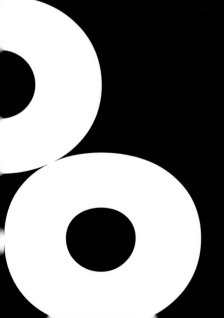

The Panda Bear Is Everyone's Life Goals; They Just Don't Know It Yet

Ask someone what animal reflects their personality and you'll probably hear answers like a lion for courage or an owl for wisdom or maybe a donkey for being really chill. Well, that menagerie better move over, because the only option that truly embodies the universal human spirit is the giant panda.

A napping expert, snack enthusiast, and fun-loving, life-of-the-party kind of mammal, the panda represents the most relaxed and joyfully quirky versions of what we could each be. Keep reading to see which panda trait you are and which one you could pick up to reach your true panda-rific self:

1.

Giant pandas treat bamboo-munching like a full-time job with overtime, regularly dedicating ten to sixteen hours to chewing per day. Luckily, they do know the value of maintaining work-life balance and break up their demanding snack shifts with two- to three-hour-long naps, accounting for the remaining ten to twelve hours of their rough days.

2.

These committed eaters are also (mostly) vegetarians! Greens and other plant material make up 99 percent of their diet. The other 1 percent, well, let's just say that the risk of a peckish panda eating your small, furry companion is low but never zero.

3.

Ever thought to yourself, "Wow, peeing would be way better if I did it from a handstand"? If yes, then you're thinking like a panda. More specifically, you're simpatico with one that wants to mark its territory as high up a tree as possible.

4.

Pandas are the only bears that have vertical, slit-like pupils similar to cats. Unfortunately, research suggests that this does not increase their desire to chase laser pointers around or sit on computer keyboards. You know the panda handlers have tried.

5.

These giant bears "make bears" (aka poo) around forty times a day. Imagine how much easier conservation efforts would be if pandas made actual baby bears with the same enthusiasm!

All Animals Poop, but Some Are Weird about It

Poo, dookie, droppings, logs, cow pies, butt burritos: whatever you call it, poop is something that unites all living things in its stinky embrace. But the way we actually doo (doo) it? That's where some animals really pull away from the average toilet-goer and lay down some spectacular scat. Here are a few standout critters that are number one at doing number two:

- **Bat** droppings, also known as "guano," are chock-full of potassium nitrate, aka the stuff that makes explosives go BOOM! And now you'll never think of "explosive diarrhea" the same way ever again.

- **Wombats** somehow poop cube-shaped turds despite their round bootyhole. Even better, the scientists who discovered this funky feces won the 2019 Ig Nobel Prize not for biology or anatomy but, you guessed it … *physics.*

- **Birds** can poop an average of forty-eight times each day, and smaller species, like sparrows, do number two every fifteen minutes. So, this is your reminder to always be on the lookout for a fly-by pooping!

- **Sloths** dance when they defecate. Scientists call this the "squat trot" (or at least that's what we think they should name it).

- **Asian palm civet** cats' poo contains coffee beans that are prized for their "unique" flavor and sell for $100 to $600 *per pound.* What's weirder? Coffee is toxic to household cats and dogs, so the Asian palm civet cat kind of has super-kitty resistance to poison.

How Dogs Made Us Go Mutts for Puppy Dog Eyes

We've all looked into the soulful depths of a precious puppy's eyes and gone a little gooey inside. There's just something about locking eyes with a dog's uniquely loving gaze that feels warm and familiar . . . like, maybe *too* familiar? If you've ever felt the glimmer in a puppy dog's eyes spark something deep in your soul, then you are catching on to a millennia-long project of evolution.

Many of us K-9 enthusiasts know that the person-pupper duo has been the iconic partnership for about twenty thousand years, but why did centuries of domestication end up making dogs with such wonderfully wiggly eyebrows? Well, just like with any strong relationship, communication is key. Scientists found that dogs have significantly larger eyebrow muscles than their wild ancestors, and this is a big deal for humans. These strong brow muscles make it possible for both people and dogs to widen their eyes. This sounds like a simple trick, but eye widening is what makes puppy dog eyes so big, expressive, and utterly irresistible. Eyebrow movement is also an important method of communication between humans, which is probably why people unknowingly choose doggos with a similarly strong brow game. So, the next time you get an inkling that your doggy companion is playing Jedi mind tricks on you with their puppy dog eyes, just know that they are and give them everything they want!

Flying the Coop for Good: The Mysterious Disappearance of the Carolina Parakeet

The Carolina parakeet was the only parrot native to North America and was prized for its vibrant plumage and affable personality. Called *puzzi la née* (meaning "yellow head") by the Seminole people living in what is now called Florida, this golden-crowned bird would travel as far north as New York in giant migratory flocks of up to three hundred birds. The parakeets' raucous arrival was a yearly spectacle for many people living in the coastal and southern parts of the US, but by the 1940s, the birds were gone.

Officials declared the parakeet extinct in 1939 and, over eighty year later, experts are still stumped as to the abrupt disappearance. Ornithologists and other scientists have several running theories about the birds' sudden population decline, and today, we are reopening this cold case and scrutinizing three prime suspects.

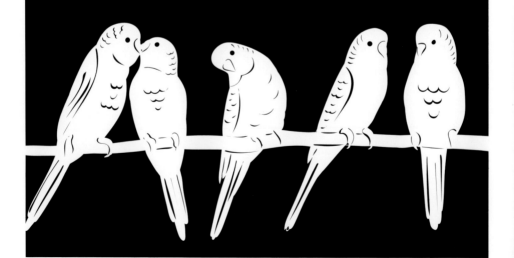

Habitat Loss

Many species of plants, animals, and insects have sadly gone the way of the dinosaur because of habitat loss, and the Carolina parakeet may be one of them. Despite their migratory patterns, the birds preferred swampy areas. One theory proposes that draining swamps for farmland led to the birds' demise. However, as shown by their wide range of migration, the birds were clearly a highly adaptable species that could have thrived elsewhere.

Human Poaching

People greatly admired the parakeets' colorful feathers and adored their sociability, maybe a little too much. Between a demand for exotic pets and exotic decorations for clothing, the bird may have been hunted to the point of extinction. But, once again, things aren't that simple. In 1913, the Weeks-McLean Act was passed to outlaw the hunting of migratory birds for commercial purposes, and other birds, like herons, came back stronger than ever before.

Avian Disease

Carolina parakeets were often attracted to crop-growing farms and possibly came into contact with domesticated fowl that carried diseases, yet there hasn't been enough research into this topic to know for sure.

In the end, our best guess is that the birds' extinction was caused by a combination of these reasons, but the mystery still puzzles the scientific community and pushes them to keep chirping, "Why?"

Parakeet Trivia to Parrot Back

1. "Parakeet" comes from the French word for parrot, which is *perroquet*. Ironically, the French word for parakeet is *perruche*.

2. The parakeet's "bird brain" is actually pretty smart! Puck the Budgerigar is one brainy bird that is on record for knowing over seventeen hundred words. That's more than a human three-year-old, who typically knows only around one thousand words.

3. Their beaks are always growing, so they have to grind them down by chewing on hard surfaces.

The Trash Panda
in Chief

The first presidential puppers to leave their paw prints on the people's lawn and hearts were President John Adams's two mixed-breed dogs, Juno and Satan. And although his taste in names was questionable, the second president's decision to bring this excellent pair of companions to the White House set the precedence for First Pets. Many furry friends have served as crucial POTUS advisors and offered their *expurrt* advice, but some have been a little more unique than others.

Rebecca the raccoon arrived at the White House during the Coolidge administration in November 1926 not as a pet but rather *as a meal*. Yes, you read that right. The story goes that some Mississippi supporters sent Coolidge the live animal as a gift for the family to eat for their Thanksgiving dinner. Thankfully, grace intervened, literally. First Lady Grace Coolidge gave the raccoon the turkey treatment and pardoned her from the dinner table. But that's just the beginning of Rebecca's memorable stay at 1600 Pennsylvania Avenue.

From that day on, Rebecca was adopted as a family pet and given a collar embroidered with "White House Raccoon." She quickly stole the spotlight and became the daily delight of both the Coolidge children and the White House Press Corps. Staffers regularly reported on the masked bandit's mischief, which often included tipping over plants, scurrying up manicured trees, and opening jars with her tiny hands to steal a little snack. Rebecca's adventures took her all over the White House grounds, but according to the First Lady, the hooligan's favorite activity was playing in the bathtub with a bar of soap.

This rambunctious raccoon continued to put in the occasional public appearance in her official capacity and rule the roost until the end of Coolidge's term in 1929. She then resigned from her high-profile position and retired to the National Zoo, where she was celebrated as the star that she undoubtedly was.

Three More Capital Critters

1. Thomas Jefferson received several bear cubs from Lewis and Clark following their return from the western exploration.

2. Having a parrot isn't unheard of, but Andrew Jackson's parrot, Poll, apparently turned heads and pricked ears with his love of curse words.

3. Known as an outdoorsy man, Theodore Roosevelt takes the cake (and maybe the entire zoo) with his menagerie of snakes, badgers, owls, pigs, zebras, lions, raccoons, and more! His kids outclassed him with the naming, though—at one point they owned five guinea pigs named Bishop Doane, Dr. Johnson, Father O'Grady, Fighting Bob Evans, and Admiral Dewey.

Free Willy
Is the New Jaws

Jaws may have ruined the ocean for generations of beach lovers, but the newest killer on the horizon is sweet little (well, big) Shamu. It turns out orcas are kind of vicious. Sailors called these oversized Oreos "whale killers" after seeing them attack a blue whale, the largest animal on earth, with the name inverting over time to "killer whale." The largest member of the dolphin family, theses super-smart cetaceans travel in pods and can coordinate their hunting tactics like a wolf pack. And whales aren't the only thing orcas hunt. These apex predators have been known to eat everything from seals and porpoises to sharks and tuna.

Found in every ocean, orcas can grow as long as thirty-two feet and weigh nearly twenty-two thousand pounds. Despite their size, they are strong enough to swim as fast at thirty-five miles per hour and to launch themselves fifteen feet out of the water. Plus they have forty to fifty sharp, three-inch-long, interlocking teeth, just the thing for ripping and tearing flesh. Their breathing is not automatic, so they never fully sleep! They keep one eye open and half of their brain conscious at all times, like deep-sea zombies.

One terrifying example of their hunting prowess can be found off the coast of South Africa. A pair of orcas learned that they could use their powerful tails to flip a shark, which causes "tonic immobility," or a trancelike state. They then eat the shark's most nutritious organ, its liver, leaving the rest of its body to rot in the sea. In a single day in March 2023, they killed nineteen sevengill sharks this way. And this is not an isolated incident—two orcas killed at least eight great white sharks in the same area six years before. No wonder sharks have been known to abandon feeding grounds the second orcas appear.

While there has been no recorded instance of an orca killing a person in the wild (although they have in captivity), they seem to be getting increasingly ticked off at the human race. (Not entirely unfair with climate change and all.) Between the coasts of Spain and Portugal, groups of killer whales have been ramming boats in increasing numbers since 2020. More than 350 incidents have occurred, with three boats sinking and one in five attacks damaging the boats so badly they couldn't move. What has turned these killer whales into Moby Dick?

Some scientists believe that orcas are learning the behavior from each other, beginning with one grandmother they've named "White Gladis." They think she might have had a run-in with a boat, and her violent reaction has been learned by others in her pod. (This kind of makes us love this feminist granny who is *done* with boats violating her space.) The attacks follow a pattern, with the orcas typically charging the rudder and losing interest once they've stopped the boat.

One night in May 2023, one large and two small orcas hit a yacht off the coast of Spain. "The little ones shook the rudder at the back while the big one repeatedly backed up and rammed the ship with full force from the side," skipper Werner Schaufelberger told *Yacht*. He then saw the smaller orcas imitate the larger one. "The two little orcas observed the bigger one's technique and, with a slight run-up, they too slammed into the boat."

Then a similar attack was
recorded off the coast of Scotland,
two thousand miles away from the
Spanish pod. Scientists are surprised,
as this incident was probably not learned
behavior because of the distance. It may be
due to a number of factors, such as dwindling
food sources, increased boat traffic, and noise.
Others think the orcas want to race the boats.

Either way, it might be time to replace the great
white shark with the killer whale as the most
terrifying creature of the deep.

A Petite History of Some Particularly Persistent Penguin Pioneers

Their bodies are round, their legs aren't designed for distance, and yet penguins have successfully settled in Africa not once, not twice, but *three times*. Although black-footed penguins rule the continent today, archeologists have dug up the fossils of four other species of penguins that made up the first and second waves of penguin pioneering. These fossilized fowl are all now extinct, and the oldest bones date back as far as thirty million years ago!

So, why did the ancient penguins disappear, and how did they keep coming back to Africa? The first answer is more of a guess. Scientists think that lower sea levels may have changed the early penguins' habitat too much. For example, South Africa would have had way more tiny islands for the birds to safely lay their eggs away from munchy predators, but receding water levels meant fewer, larger islands. The second answer is also water related but way easier to prove. Describing the ocean's natural currents as "penguin conveyor belts," researchers are confident that the birds kept showing up because they just washed up from time to time. This is how these watery nomads can be found all over the globe, including Australia, South America, and of course, Antarctica. So, really, when surf's up, you can always count on a penguin to go with the flow.

Three More Waddle-y Facts about Our Wayward Wanderers

1. The little blue penguin is the smallest type of penguin, coming in at thirteen inches high and weighing only three pounds. Their petite stature is why they're also called little penguins or, the best thing you'll read all day: fairy penguins.

2. Scientist can't decide how many species of penguins there are. The range is between seventeen and twenty, but people are split about whether or not some kinds, like rockhoppers, are actually their own species.

3. Before the name "penguin" was created, some explorers just called them "strange geese." To be fair, what is any bird but a strange type of goose?

Narlugas Are the Unicorns of Unicorns

If you've ever wondered whether unicorns exist, just ask Lars Jensen. Jensen was an Inuit subsistence hunter who pulled in a puzzling catch off the waters near Disko Bay in West Greenland in the late 1980s. Although he and his community had been hunting narwhals and beluga whales for millennia, he had never seen one . . . of . . . these. Weirder still, he had three of them.

The animals had the flippers of a beluga but the tail of a narwhal. They weren't completely white like a beluga or mottled gray like a narwhal—they were smooth gray all over. Inuit hunters had known about an animal like this for some time, but they were extremely rare and Jensen had never seen one before.

Whatever it was, Jensen knew it was a prize catch, and so he mounted one of the skulls on the roof of his shed. It remained there until one day in 1990, when Mads Peter Heide-Jørgensen, a marine scientist, spotted it. He asked Jensen if whether he could borrow this bizarre-looking skull, and he took it to Copenhagen for study at the Greenland Fisheries Research Institute.

Heide-Jørgensen hypothesized that it was a hybrid between a narwhal and a beluga whale, but with no way to prove it, the skull remained shrouded in mystery for nearly thirty years. In 2019, Eline Lorenzen, an evolutionary biologist at the Natural History Museum of Denmark, finally confirmed what we had all hoped for: the narluga is real, and it's an oddly lovable beast.

Lorenzen was able to determine from the DNA that the animal had been a male narluga, with a beluga father and a narwhal mother. Narwhals and beluga whales are the only two living members of the species Monodontidae (the other four are now extinct), but they've evolved independently of each other for over one million years. No one knows why they would mate or how often it happens, since the narwhal and the beluga are not really as compatible as you might think.

For one, the narwhal male has that slightly noticeable ivory tusk protruding from its head, which can be up to ten feet long and weigh twenty-two pounds. (This spiraling tusk is actually a canine tooth, and it protrudes from its upper lip, not its head. But it's still the "unicorn of the sea" in our hearts.) It uses this tooth/horn to slap and stun fish, attract mates, and possibly even detect changes in salinity, temperature, and pressure in the water through its thousands of nerve endings. On the other hand, the beluga has a bulbous forehead (called a "melon"), and it can change the shape of its head by blowing air around its sinuses. Points for a cool party trick, but still not a unicorn horn … sorry, friend.

For two, the mouth of a narwhal is very different from the mouth of a beluga. A narwhal is virtually toothless. It has its tusk, which spirals counterclockwise, and a small pair of vestigial teeth behind it. But when you open its mouth, there's absolutely nothing. "The whole thing that is great about the teeth of the narwhal is that nothing makes sense," says Martin Nweeia, a practicing dentist and member of the Smithsonian's Department of Vertebrate Zoology. Because of this, the narwhal has to stun fish with its tusk, then suction them completely whole with its mouth.

On the other side of the table, beluga whales have up to forty teeth in both their upper and lower jaws, all identical, all uniform, and just plain sensible. They bite; they chew; they eat all the same things narwhals eat, but with what you might call table manners.

Now, the narluga, innovator that it is, looked at these two options and decided to go its own way. It has eighteen teeth inside of its mouth, all different, all crooked, all confusing. Some are long and pointy, some are short and flat, some are sticking out horizontally, and some even spiral to the left, like a narwhal tusk.

By analyzing these teeth, Lorenzen's team was able to determine that the narluga couldn't possibly have eaten what its parents ate. Both narwhals and belugas eat halibut, cod, squid, and shrimp, but because of its kooky teeth, the narluga had to hunt more like a bottom-feeder—trolling the ocean floor with its crooked rake mouth to dig up prey buried in the sand. If you're the only you in the world, this is completely acceptable.

You might be asking: how could they possibly have missed the opportunity to call it a belwhal? The name "narluga" is actually one of the few species portmanteaus that punts at the patriarchy. As climate change has radically altered habitats so that species that would not have crossed paths (such as grizzly and polar bears) are now overlapping in terrain, hybrid animals are becoming more common. Think of these as the mash-ups man made.

In these cases, scientists have traditionally followed the convention that the father's species be named before the mother's. So, if a male polar bear and a female grizzly mate, their offspring is a pizzly, whereas a male grizzly and a female polar bear would make a grolar. According to this custom, the skull Lorenzen identified is, in fact, a belwhal. But as she said, and we agree, narluga just sounds better.

Unfortunately, we're not likely to have a whole stable of narlugas to coo at any time soon. Narwhals are incredibly elusive and don't do well in captivity, so little is known about them and their habits. They spend most of their lives under the Arctic ice, where extreme temperatures and little or no daylight make them difficult to track and study.

Their fate depends on the ice, which is rapidly shrinking. But they also need breathing holes, which the Inuit call "sassats," and when climate change causes sudden shifts in winds and temperatures, many can freeze completely, leaving them without enough breathing holes to get them to open sea. They then crowd into one rapidly shrinking breathing hole, where they suffocate and die while fighting for air. In 1915, the largest entrapment ever seen was recorded, when nearly one thousand narwhals were trapped under the ice in West Greenland. Although these entrapments have always been part of the hard life of living in the Arctic, their frequency appears to be increasing as the Arctic warms.

As for the narluga, it's unknown whether the one Jensen found was fertile and could have contributed to declining population numbers. Most hybrids are infertile, making them genetic dead ends and creating another obstacle for the species as a whole. If it were fertile, then it could potentially have helped the species by increasing genetic diversity, which is extremely low in narwhals. The population of narwhals is thought to be up to 170,000, putting them in the "near-threatened" category created by the International Union for Conservation of Nature.

In December 2021, a lone male narwhal was spotted living with a pod of male beluga whales, clearly having been adopted into the pod. If these gents come across a pod of beluga females and the light and the water are *just* right, we may soon have our next narluga baby. And a baby unicorn-of-the-sea might just be the supernova of cuteness our worlds need.

More Odd Facts about Our Odd Friends

Narwhals live up to ninety years, and they can weigh as much as 3,500 pounds. They live in the Arctic and Atlantic oceans surrounding Greenland, Canada, Norway, and Russia.

Narwhals are named after the Old Norse word *nahvalr*, or "corpse-whale," because they were thought to look like the bodies of dead sailors.

Both female and male narwhals have two canine teeth emerging from their skulls, but only in males does the left tooth grow nine to ten feet long. About one in five hundred males has two tusks, and about 3 percent of females have a small tusk.

Narwhals have made some of the deepest dives ever recorded, up to one mile deep, and they can stay underwater without surfacing for air for over twenty-five minutes. The pressure at this depth is the equivalent of 150 atmospheres, but because they have compressible rib cages and a high concentration of oxygen-binding myoglobin, they can still swim up to three feet per second during these vertical dives.

According to Inuit myths, the narwhal was once a woman with long hair that she braided to look like a tusk. But she was cruel to her blind son, so he tied her to a white whale, and she drowned and was ultimately transformed into a narwhal. According to the myth, he felt sort of bad but also thought it was worth it, because she had been pretty unkind.

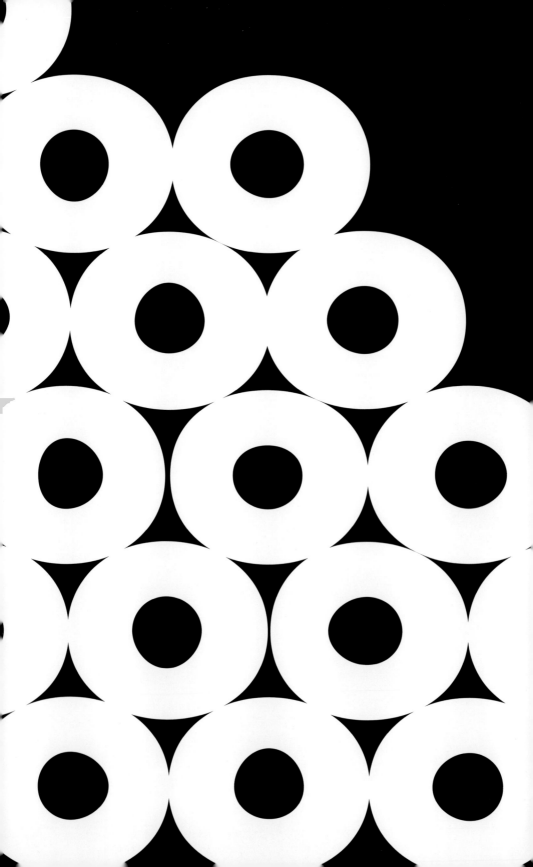

2

Culture Curios
from the Basement

Well, Actually . . . It's Time to Fact-Check Your Friends

We hate to say it, but sometimes there's nothing more satisfying than dropping a perfectly timed "Well, actually . . ." on the right person. To increase your opportunities to make a tactful correction, we've compiled a list of common "facts" about history that are actually FALSE. (Yes, you can shout "FALSE" in the person's face while correcting them.) Remember, with great trivia knowledge comes great irresponsibility.

 The infamous quote "Let them eat cake" was not only misattributed to Marie Antoinette but also said *one hundred years before her*. The quote actually belongs to a different French royal, Marie-Thérèse, who was the queen consort to King Louis XIV.

 Ninjas wore navy, not black. This misconception has been traced back to a play written for a Japanese Kabuki theater when a writer had a ninja character disguise themselves as a stagehand. Just like today, stagehands typically wore black, so the idea that ninjas also wore black spread as the show was repeated other places.

 "Pandora's box" is a mistranslation of "Pandora's jar." The translation error happened hundreds of years ago and unleashed its own translation chaos upon the world ever since.

Gladiators didn't always fight to the death. Promoters put in a lot of money to scout and train fighters, so in reality, fatalities happened only 10 to 20 percent of the time. That number still isn't low enough for *us* to get in the ring, but it is way lower than most people think!

 Napoleon Bonaparte wasn't a short king. Yes, he was technically five feet, two inches, but this height was based on France's prerevolutionary measurement system. According to US standards, Bonaparte was five feet, six inches, which was actually one inch taller than the average French man at the time.

Giving Flowers and Passing Notes: The Covert Messaging System of Floriography

Flower choice can mean a lot of things, like a rose for love, a lily for condolences, or a bouquet of three roses, a carnation, and a chrysanthemum to say "laugh out loud." Wait, what? Taking inspiration from the art of floriography, some modern-day florists have taken this clandestine messaging system and updated the code to send some pretty funny (and vaguely threatening) messages. But what is floriography exactly, and where did it come from before reappearing as a new and popular gift-giving gimmick?

Floriography literally means "the language of flowers," but more technically speaking, it's a type of cryptologic communication that assigns certain meanings to individual flowers or floral arrangements. Although this floral code sprouted thousands of years ago, it was really popularized in mainstream culture during the nineteenth century by the Victorians, because of course. Their fascination with the language of flowers eventually cross-pollinated with American culture, and soon both countries had their noses buried in "floral dictionaries." Exchanging "talking bouquets" was quickly (and unsurprisingly) used for mostly one thing: flirting. Also known as tussie-mussies, these encoded arrangements were carried as an accessory or even worn on the person's clothes. Talk about wearing your heart on your sleeve!

- **Apple blossom:** Fame speaks them great and good.

- **Bud of white rose:** Your heart is ignorant of love.

- **Chinese chrysanthemum:** Stay cheerful in the face of adversity!

- **Japanese rose:** Beauty is your only attraction.

- **Milk vetch:** Your presence makes my hardships bearable.

- **Peaches:** Your charms and qualities are unequaled.

- **Queen's rocket:** You're a true fashionista.

- **Wild tansy:** I declare war on you!

Drink Pepsi, Win a Fighter Jet

In the 1990s, Pepsi launched its biggest campaign ever: "Drink Pepsi, Get Stuff." By collecting labels, fans could accumulate points that could be turned in for prizes like a Pepsi-branded hat, T-shirt, mountain bike, or jean jacket. Seems straightforward, right?

But then Pepsi made the mistake of trying to be funny. In one commercial, a kid landed at his school in an AV-8 Harrier II jump jet, with a price tag of seven million Pepsi Points flashing on the screen. Sure, it seemed like a joke. Who could drink seventeen million sodas to get that many points? But a college student named John Leonard didn't see it that way.

A business major, Leonard realized the military aircraft was worth $33.8 million and would be a bargain at the Pepsi Points price. So he put together a business plan outlining how he could monetize the jet and started looking for investors. Then Pepsi made their second mistake: the contest rules stated that, once a consumer had fifteen Pepsi Points, they could buy points for ten cents each … meaning the seven million points Leonard needed for the jet would cost "only" $700,000. A steal!

At that price, his business plan attracted five investors, including a millionaire named Todd Hoffman who met Leonard on a mountaineering trip. Hoffman was the tipping point to the jet-buying scheme. Leonard later said that Pepsi was "counting on there being a ton of dreamers like me, but they just never figured a dreamer like me would ever have access to somebody that was willing to go on this crazy ride and actually would write the check."

Leonard sent in the necessary fifteen Pepsi Points and a check for the balance and waited for the response. The company returned the check with a note saying the jet in the commercial was "fanciful and is simply included to create a humorous and entertaining ad." Pepsi condescendingly threw in some coupons for free soda. But by this time, Leonard had already paid $4,000 to research deceptive advertising, so he wasn't going to be bought off with a few six-packs of Pepsi. Instead, he hired an attorney to sue the company.

When confronted with the lawsuit, Pepsi could have turned Leonard's quest into a funny story about a young entrepreneur's moxie. But instead, they sicced a team of corporate lawyers on him, making what should have been a small situation into a big deal. After newspapers all over the county picked up the story, Pepsi offered Leonard a $750,000 settlement to go away, which he promptly turned down. Leonard was holding out for the jet.

Not surprisingly, a judge eventually ruled that a television commercial is not a contractually binding offer. She stated that the setup was clearly in jest, writing, "The notion of traveling to school in a Harrier Jet is an exaggerated adolescent fantasy." Pepsi tried to cover their butt by changing the commercial: the jet was now seven hundred million points, with the words "Just Kidding" next to it.

"Looking back on it, it was opportunistic. Absolutely. But that's not always a negative thing," Leonard later told the *Guardian*. "And back then I wholeheartedly thought that we were going to get the jet." But as decades have passed, Leonard said he had to ask himself the question, "What kind of idiot were you?"

The Pioneering Filmmaker You've Never Seen

The early history of cinema was dominated by dudes making boring movies. Think Eadweard Muybridge's series photography of a galloping horse. Thomas Edison's kinetoscope of a guy sneezing. The Lumiere brothers' Cinematographe film of workers leaving a factory. Not exactly riveting storytelling. Stepping into this void was Alice Guy-Blaché.

As a child, Alice traveled all over the world, bouncing among her grandmother's house in Switzerland to her mother in France to her father in Chile. After her father died, she began working to support her family. At twenty-two, Alice became a secretary for Léon Gaumont, whose company sold motion-picture cameras. Movies were so new that the company made short, medium-boring films of everyday life to demonstrate how the camera worked.

While Alice had no theatrical experience beyond some amateur plays, she knew she could make better films (who couldn't?). When she asked Gaumont, he replied, "It seems like a silly, girlish thing to do." But he agreed to let her try, as long as it didn't affect her office work.

Alice's first motion picture, *The Cabbage Fairy*, was made in 1896. The silent film was only about one minute long, but it had costumes, a painted set, and a brief story about a fairy placing babies in a cabbage patch. Sure, it was no *Lord of the Rings*, but her boss was charmed.

Over the next ten years, Alice made hundreds of films, which included a thirty-minute silent film about the life of Jesus Christ that had interior and exterior shots and hundreds of extras. She also directed, produced, or supervised nearly 150 synchronized sound films for the

company's Chronophone division. But it wasn't easy. "My youth, my inexperience, my sex all conspired against me," she later wrote. (No kidding—in France, women didn't get the right to work without getting permission from their husbands until 1965!)

In 1907, Alice gave up her job and moved to America with her new husband and fellow Gaumont employee, Herbert Blaché. He was tasked with starting a Chronophone franchise in Cleveland, but it was a flop. Herbert was then sent to head up the Gaumont studio. But rival filmmaker Thomas Edison (who was a surprisingly ruthless businessman) used his influence to thwart the company's expansion in the US. So the studio often sat idle.

In 1910, Alice decided to take advantage of that downtime, and she started her own production company, Solax. Over the next few years, she made more than six hundred dramas, action movies, and comedies of all types in the Gaumont studio, eventually opening her own studio in Fort Lee, New Jersey, in 1912. The glass-roofed, state-of-the-art studio had prop and dressing rooms, five stage sets, and a carpentry workshop.

Alice's films stressed natural acting, not the stilted drama of other silent films. She also was ahead of her time in casting, employing women as action stars doing their own stunts or in marriages where the partners were equal. This approach reflected her life, where in addition to being a mother of two and running her own studio, Alice also scouted locations, managed hundreds of adult and child actors, and had a slew of animal performers, including a six-hundred-pound tiger named Princess. The industry's eventual shift to the West Coast and rising costs, however, meant many East Coast studios had to close, including Solax.

For a while, Alice and Herbert directed films for other studios, but the couple eventually separated. Herbert moved to Hollywood. Alice rejoined him briefly after nearly dying from the Spanish flu, but he had already moved on to dating actresses (real original, Herb). They divorced in 1920, the year Alice made her last film, *Tarnished Reputations.*

Alice returned with her children to France in 1922. Due to changes in the film industry, she was unable to get work and instead supported herself writing stories, and she eventually moved back to New Jersey to live with her daughter. When Alice died, she was buried in the same state where she blazed a trail by being the only woman to own a movie studio—a fact still true to this day.

Christmas 1977's Hottest Toy? An Empty Cardboard Box

When *Star Wars* opened on May 25, 1977, few people thought it was going to be a hit. Not the director, George Lucas, who booked a trip to Hawaii on the opening weekend to avoid the bad press. Not 20th Century Fox, which initially released the movie onto a measly forty-two screens. Not actress Carrie Fisher, who thought Princess Leia in the little science fiction movie would soon be forgotten.

With many fearing a box-office bomb, it was no surprise that the Kenner toy company didn't put a lot of effort into the merchandise. They planned a few easy-to-produce but lame items like puzzles and coloring books. So when the movie turned out to be a smash hit with lines around the block, they were caught flat-footed. How could they quickly cash in on being the license holder to the biggest movie of the year?

Fans were clamoring for action figures. But at the time, it took a year of development to design, sculpt, test, and create steel molds. Even if the company worked nonstop, there was no way Kenner would have action figures ready in time for the prime holiday selling season.

Scrambling to find some way to release anything, Brad Loomis, an executive at the toy company, came up with a crazy idea. What if they created an "Early Bird Certificate Package," which would guarantee that fans would receive the company's first four action figures: Luke Skywalker, Princess Leia, R2-D2, and Chewbacca?

The force that is *Star Wars* compelled thousands of people to buy a practically empty cardboard box for $7.99. Inside was a certificate, some stickers, a *Star Wars* fan club card, a picture of the twelve-figure line that was to come the following spring, and the ability to turn the box into a display for the figures that currently didn't exist. Kenner even had the audacity to limit the sale to five hundred thousand boxes, with none to be sold after December 31.

Kenner's marketing ploy worked. Kids all over the country happily received that nearly empty box on Christmas morning. Collectors savvy enough not to rip open their Early Bird Certificate Package found themselves with a hunk of cardboard that would later sell for thousands of dollars. And the toy company learned their lesson—they went on to produce more than one hundred different action figures, enough to satisfy fans of even the most obscure characters.

So 20th Century Fox must have been thrilled with the revenue generated by the toy line, right? Not really, as they didn't see a single penny. There hadn't been a lot of enthusiasm for the film when they negotiated with creator George Lucas. So in exchange for a lower fee for direction, Lucas retained the sequel rights and all of the merchandising rights. Over the next year, Kenner would sell nearly forty million figures, making Lucas a very wealthy man.

The original *Star Wars*, which was later renamed *Episode IV: A New Hope*, grossed $550 million in its initial run and won seven Oscars. The media franchise has since become ridiculously lucrative with estimated merchandise sales of $20 billion, making Lucas the richest movie director in history.

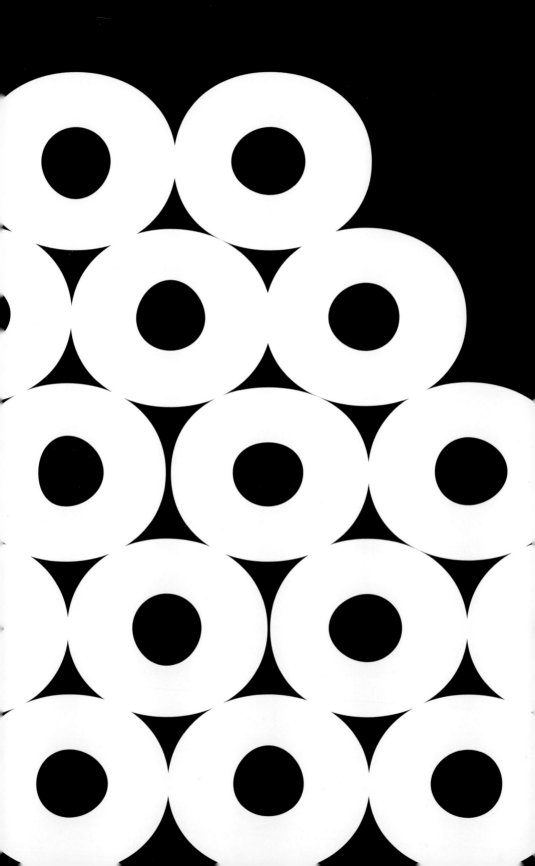

3

Food Facts for Your Indigestion

"Ring-around-the-Crab-Salad" and Four Other Jell-O-atinous Culinary Crimes

The 1960s were the peak of all things groovy and experimental. Hippies roamed free, music was psychedelic, and plates were piled high with . . . Jell-O?

Filled to the gills with fish, fruit, and fillings best left in a salad, Jell-O experienced its main character moment as the go-to ingredient for seemingly any dish during the sixties. Shockingly, these concoctions eventually fell out of popular taste (oh no!), but their recipes still live on. These are a few that truly broke the mold:

1.
Tomato aspic

Lemon-flavored Jell-O infused with tomato juice, hot sauce, and vinegar; this dish may be too gruesome even for Bloody Mary herself. Oh, and don't forget the green olive and cucumber accoutrement.

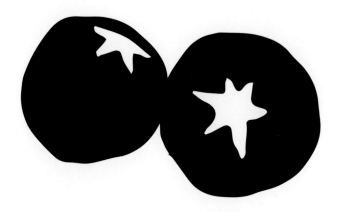

2.
Vegetable trio

Straight out of Popeye's dreams (or nightmares?), the vegetable trio is a triple layered Jell-O loaf made of—you guessed it—three delectable superfoods: spinach, cucumber, and carrot. Garnish your veg bar with cilantro for a sweet treat that can't be beet, literally.

3.
Seafood salad bowl

Ever thought that a crab salad was just *too* boring? Well, neither have we. Truly a hero without a cause, Jell-O ruins the day once again with this blobfish of a bowl. It's a smorgasbord of grapefruit and celery leaves suspended in a ring of lime Jell-O and topped with mayo. Yet more proof that "creative" does not always mean "good" or "edible."

4.
Fall fruit soufflé

Move over pumpkin spice lattes—there's a new seasonal sensation in town. Picture this: A heaping cup of mayonnaise. Coat that with lime Jell-O. Add walnuts for crunch and grapes for color, mix, chill, and bam! You have a dish that will make you question everything you thought you knew about festive fall flavors.

5.
The "perfection salad"

Nothing screams *HELP!*—oops, we mean "dinner party showstopper"—like a coagulated column of pickled cabbage, tomatoes, cucumbers, onions, and carrots. Dessert meets antipasto, this lemon Jell-O plus vinegar abomination brings together the worst of all possible worlds.

Eight Apple Facts
That Are Good to the Core

Whether you like them red or green, sweet or tart, apples have been our go-to fruit for the last 8,500 years, according to archeological findings. The average American alone eats about sixteen pounds of apples each year, which goes to show that our love for this crisp treat is still strong as ever. Here are eight apple-aud-worthy facts that will make you see the fruit's a-peel even more.

1.

Apples are originally from Kazakhstan and were one of the many products that spread around the world via the Silk Road.

2.

Did you know that there's a science to growing the perfect apple? It's called pomology!

3.

A bushel of apples weighs 42 pounds while a peck comes in at 10.5 pounds. That means that loving someone "a bushel and a peck" totals up to 52.5 pounds of apple-solute affection!

4.

Washington State grows enough apples every year to wrap around the globe not once, not twice, but *twenty-nine times*.

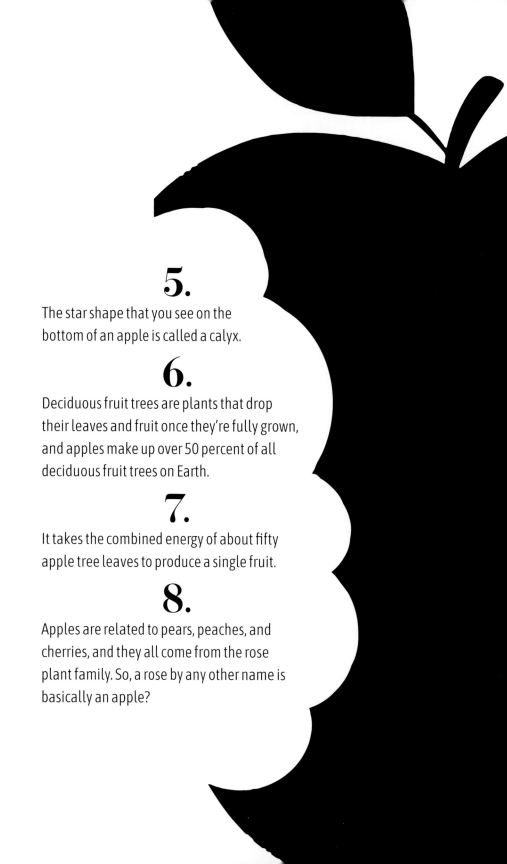

5.

The star shape that you see on the bottom of an apple is called a calyx.

6.

Deciduous fruit trees are plants that drop their leaves and fruit once they're fully grown, and apples make up over 50 percent of all deciduous fruit trees on Earth.

7.

It takes the combined energy of about fifty apple tree leaves to produce a single fruit.

8.

Apples are related to pears, peaches, and cherries, and they all come from the rose plant family. So, a rose by any other name is basically an apple?

How One City Put the "Radish" in "Holiday T-radish-ion"

'Twas the night before Christmas, and everybody was eating a radish. Wait. What? Yes, someone, somewhere, decided to link Christmas with these little pink root vegetables, and now there's no going back for any of us. The Night of the Radishes is a spooky-sounding festival that celebrates this crisp veggie on the night before, and the night before the night before, Christmas. To get to the root (vegetable) of this eyebrow-raising combination, we need to dust off our gardening trowels and dig a little deeper into some Mexican history.

Located in the southern region of Mexico, the city of Oaxaca began carving radishes every December 23 into elaborate dioramas and fantastical sculptures *over 125 years ago*, but the seeds of this t-radish-ional Christmas holiday go back even further. (Fun fact: radishes aren't actually native to North America at all but were brought over to Mexico by Spanish settlers during the 1500s.) At the time, Oaxaca was a small city with nutrient-dense farmland. And when we say "nutrient dense," we mean like, "Oh, no. We've accidentally grown radishes the size of newborn babies" kind of dense.

That's right—the city had so many radishes by the mid-eighteenth century that farmers just started leaving them in the field one spring season because what could possibly go wrong? Well, everyone found out when they came back the following December (aka Christmastime) to clean up the stragglers but discovered monstrously huge and irregularly shaped blobs instead. Apparently, like the goldfish of the veggie world, it turns out that these once bite-sized morsels can actually grow up to 30 inches long (80 centimeters) and frequently over 6.5 pounds (3 kilograms) with enough time and space.

These giga roots (obviously) became a town spectacle and (less obviously) inspired a few woodcarvers to turn the radishes into nativity scenes to celebrate the holiday season. Nowadays, the yearly festival features a diverse body of work, ranging from miniature mariachi bands to delicate flowers to elaborate dragons. All the displays are part of a competition to choose the most impressive entry, but we can't help rooting for them all!

Trivia That Puts the "Rad" in Radish

1. Radishes are originally from China and are close relatives with another Asian root vegetable, Japanese wasabi.

2. They can grow tiny white- or purple-lined flowers! We usually don't get to see them because radishes are typically harvested before they can bloom.

3. We grow about seven million tons of radishes a year, which is a lot, but this number makes up only 2 percent of all produce grown per year.

The Explosive Invention of Cheese Curls

Notorious for staining fingers and possessing almost zero nutritional value, cheese curls might be the most pointless food ever invented, and that's why we love them. But this corny emotional support snack didn't always exist, despite the fact that humans have been growing corn for over 10,000 years. (That's right—that's 10,000 years where not one person figured out that corn could curl.) Instead, they are the product of the tireless innovation, precise engineering, and . . . an accidental explosion at a horse feed manufacturer? Although this origin story is far from the epic beginning we had in mind, it's definitely the cheesiest accident that the snack-food industry could have ever hoped for.

The origin story of our favorite cheese-flavored puff first takes us to a bustling city of thirty-seven thousand people: Beloit, Wisconsin. Like many other midwestern locales, Beloit is part of Wisconsin's agricultural hub and home to several processing plants, like the Flakall Corporation (aka inventor of the cheese puff). Before they struck puffed gold in the 1930s, the Beloit-based manufacturing plant focused their innovative and production efforts on making animal feed from corn. Flakall machines turned grains of corn into flakes, which optimized the amount of feed produced and also made it safer for their future furry customers to eat without the risk of being jabbed in the snoot with a sharp corn kernel. The business was tootin' along, and everything was dandy . . . until one day, while cleaning, a bit of wet corn accidentally came into direct contact with the hottest part of the machine. *BOOM!* Puffs as far as the eye could see. From there, all it took was one inventive and munchy employee to take some of the byproduct home, spice it up, and rebrand the accidental waste as "Korn Kurls" for the cheese curls to be born.

A Few More Cheese Puff Facts to Snack On

- According to PepsiCo (aka Frito-Lay's parent company), it takes an army of five thousand cows producing eleven million gallons of milk to make a year's worth of Cheeto Puffs.

- An unusually large cheese puff once almost sold on eBay for over $1 million. The auction was shut down before the ultimate bid was chosen, but the owner of the puff eventually donated it to a town in Iowa to become a tourist attraction.

- Another early name for cheese puffs was "CheeWees," which (thankfully) didn't stick around.

- The current world record for the greatest number of cheese puffs eaten in twenty seconds is thirteen puffs. We're not saying that we could beat that ourselves, but we're also not *not* saying it either.

Spilling the Tea: Why the History of Boba Is Steeped in Controversy

Beloved for its iconic combination of milky black tea and addictively chewy tapioca balls, Taiwanese bubble tea (or "boba tea") has undeniably taken the world by storm since its invention in the 1980s. In fact, a study done in 2020 projected that the bubble tea industry will grow by $2 billion and become worth nearly $5 billion by 2027. But as you'll soon find out, reading the tea leaves to predict the drink's future is way easier than figuring out where it really came from. The true origins of bubble tea are actually steeped in mystery, and we've collected a few leading theories for you to tea-se out.

The Chun Shui Tang Tea House Theory

One of the most popular theories circles around a Taiwanese tea house, Chun Shui Tang, that was thirsty for innovation. Before coming up with their big boba idea, the shop first made the daring choice to serve iced tea after the business's founder returned from a trip to

Japan, where he tried something that you might have heard about: "iced coffee." Fast-forward to 1988, when an employee brings a new type of bouncy candy called "fen yuan" into the shop and jokingly drops it into a glass of iced milk tea. Of course, that candy was boba pearls, and the rest is history . . . or at least it's one version of it.

The Hanlin Tea House Theory

Another well-known origin story begins with a story about failure. Shortly following the devastating failure of a business venture in 1986, entrepreneur Tu Tsong He was himself brewing over his next move when inspiration struck: he would open a tea house! Coincidentally, this tea lover was *also* a big fan of fen yuan, just like the employee in our previous story (hmm, interesting). In an interview with CNN, Tu Tsong He retold his eureka moment, saying, "I thought to myself, 'Why don't I add some fen yuan into my green tea?'" And *BAM*, that's how boba tea was (maybe) born.

But Which One Is True?

These accounts finally collided as a boiling-hot lawsuit between the tea houses, both of which wanted to patent the increasingly popular drinkable snack (or snackable drink?). A decision wasn't made until 2019, when a court decided that boba tea was a general food item and couldn't be patented, which made both parties' claims about inventing the drink kind of irrelevant. So, in the end, you're the real winner because you can believe in either story and enjoy your bubble tea worry-free.

Quali-tea Boba Facts to Chew On

- Although we don't really know whether Tu Tsong invented bubble tea first, he is usually credited for referring to the drink's tapioca balls as "pearls" first. The word came to him because the tapioca balls (which were white in his original version of the drink) reminded him of his mother's pearls.

- The "bubble" in bubble tea isn't describing the boba pearls! It's actually a reference to the foam that collects on top of the drink when you shake it.

- The chewy treat is enjoyed in over thirty different countries worldwide and has even been sold by major chains, like when McDonald's sold boba in eight hundred of their German locations in 2012.

Why Your Coffee
Is Probably Contraband

It's the early 1600s in the Middle East, and you spot a pilgrim who is on their way to India. Typically, seeing another pilgrim wouldn't earn a second glace, but this man is constantly looking over his shoulder as though he's on the run. His name is Baba Budan, and one day we'll find out that he was traveling with something that would revolutionize life as we know it forever: six tiny coffee beans.

Baba Budan's story is the first known instance of what would become a long history of coffee smuggling. The few beans that smugglers like Budan stole would spread across the globe and eventually grow into one of the biggest commodities in the modern world. You're probably wondering, isn't 1600 kind of recent? The answer: absolutely yes!

Although the coffee bean's origins are traced back to tenth-century Ethiopia, the plant was limited to parts of the Middle East and Africa for another seven hundred years. Why? Because the Ottomans knew that they had struck black gold from their first sip and went to extreme measures to control supply. In fact, no beans were allowed to leave the empire unless they had been boiled or partially roasted first, two processes that stopped the beans from growing.

Of course, as word spread about this wonder plant and of successful smuggling operations, more and more people tried to get in on the action, like the Dutch, the French, and others. Sailors transported the stolen goods to other places where the beans could grow, like Brazil, which caused the coffee boom of 1822. So, now you know exactly what to say when the non-coffee-drinkers around you think the PSL life is a brand new level of caffeine craze.

Perpetual Stew: The Soup That's Always On

What do honey, dried beans, powdered milk, and a fifty-year-old Thai beef soup all have in common? They will most definitely, probably never expire, maybe! One restaurant in Bangkok takes "the expiration date is just a suggestion" to the next level with their world-famous perpetual stew that has been simmering and feeding people continuously since 1974.

Originally put on (and never taken off) over fifty years ago, Wattana Panich's beef and goat noodle soup has been cultivated and maintained by the same family for three generations. The soup is seasoned with pepper, cilantro root, cinnamon, garlic, and roughly a dozen other Chinese herbs. Patrons say that the soup's flavor is "hard to explain" but meaty and fragrant. But we know what you're wondering: how?

Like the stew equivalent of the ship of Theseus, just a little bit of the soup is saved at the end of each day and simmered overnight. Wattana Panich's chefs then use that reduction as the base for the next day's giant batch of brew. So, yes, the broth has *technically* been cooking since the 1970s, but it's lovingly fed and has been aged like a fine wine or, in this case, a fine soup!

Three More Soup Facts to Stew On

1. Maybe the pinnacle of human narcissism, one French king once commanded his chefs to make him a soup that he could look into and admire his own reflection. Thus, consommé, or clear broth, was introduced to the world.

2. The earliest signs of humans eating soup dates back to over six thousand years ago, but can you guess what kind it was? If your answer was hippopotamus, then you are correct and probably a trivia master!

3. It is illegal in the great state of Nebraska for bars to sell beer if there's no soup on to boil. We don't know why this is, but we do think that this should become a nationwide policy ASAP.

How Bananas Nearly Gave Us the Slip, Permanently

From Andy Warhol's art to friendship-ending races in Mario Kart, the banana is a staple in more places than just the kitchen. This brilliantly yellow fruit has become a major part of our daily lives, but in an alternate world not far from our own, bananas would have gone extinct by the end of the 1900s.

The pivotal intervention that saved the banana was prompted by a disease that began overtaking the global banana crop in the 1950s. Also called "banana wilt," Panama disease is caused by a fungus that spreads through the soil and infects the entire fruit-bearing plant. This particular outbreak moved quickly and almost completely wiped out the dominant species of commercial bananas at that time, the Gros Michel.

Just like other plants, the banana plant has several different varieties. The version of the fruit that we're all bananas for today is called the Cavendish, but the Gros Michel was the modern banana's tastier and less easily bruised cousin. The Cavendish ended up becoming the new golden (yellow) child because it was resistant to the specific strain of Panama disease that was rapidly taking over. The new banana in town also had some other perks, like staying green longer for shipment and being pretty darn good-looking.

The swap was a success, and the banana-to-table supply chain was completely overhauled to accommodate the monoculture's new star.

And that's how we saved the banana for good … at least that's what we thought. Banana scientists across the globe have recently started raising alarm bells about another possible outbreak of Panama disease in the near future. So, is the banana as we know it doomed once again? Maybe, but the same experts believe that we might be able to save the banana once again, with another banana split of genes.

Even More Bananas Fruit Trivia

- According to the Food and Agriculture Organization of the United Nations, the average person eats at least three bananas every week, a rate that totals about 130 bananas a year.

- Have you ever noticed that some banana-flavored things, like taffy, don't really taste like real bananas? You're not crazy—the flavor is actually different! Companies like Laffy Taffy started making banana-flavored candy before the 1950s banana plague, so their flavors are based off a version of the fruit that we don't eat anymore.

- *Musa sapientum* is the banana's scientific name and means "fruit of the wise men."

Why Salt and Pepper
Are Accidental Soulmates

Peanut butter and jelly. Mac and cheese. Bacon and eggs. All of these are absolutely iconic food combinations, but no duo is more closely tied to Western cuisine than salt and pepper. Having salt and pepper on the table is probably such a no-brainer that few of us have ever paused while passing the pair to ask, "Wait, why is it always salt *AND* pepper?"

To start with the obvious keeper of the two, salt has and always will be a fan favorite all over the world. After all, it doesn't just enhance the flavor of food. It's also an important part of our regular bodily functions, from our muscles to our nervous systems! But pepper? This is a harder sell. While salt has always been a cooking necessity, peppercorns are relatively new to the dinner rush and owe their breakthrough to the French monarch King Louis XIV.

Also known as the Sun King, which is definitely reflective of his ego, Louis XIV ruled France from 1643 to 1715. France was a center of art, culture, and cuisine at the time, and nothing got a trend spreading around Europe like wildfire faster than the king plugging it. According to historians, this showy royal preferred his seasoning light and simple, and freshly ground salt and pepper were his regular dining companions. So, next time you're passing the salt and pepper shakers, you can thank (or blame) Louis XIV for this kind-of-random matchmaking.

Salt Facts to Taste

The word "salary" comes from the Latin word for salt, *sal*. This is because salt was once so valuable that it was used as money.

In the 1920s, people discovered that salt could be used to treat a thyroid disorder called goiter, which is caused by a deficiency of iodine. Companies started selling iodized salt and erased nearly all goiter cases.

Tears carry traces of salt—even in turtles! Sea turtles cry to flush excess salt from their bodies.

A Saccharine Tsunami
for the Ages

It was in the thick of World War I, and the United States Industrial Alcohol Company needed a place to store gooey-sweet molasses. It was a key ingredient in industrial alcohol, which was used to create explosives. So in 1915, the company quickly built a fifty-eight-foot-high holding tank at the Purity Distilling Company offices near busy Commercial Street in Boston. When it started to leak, they painted it brown to hide the stains. But children knew they could stand under the groaning tank and fill up cups with the sweet syrup that dripped from it.

In the early afternoon of January 15, 1919, nearby railroad workers loading freight cars heard what sounded like gunfire. It was the rivets as they shot off the tank. Then they heard a rumbling and the bottom of the tank burst, ripping the metal apart. Seconds later more than two million gallons of molasses were released in a giant wave. Train cars were swept away, and men working in the basement of the company drowned before they could escape.

The dense wall of syrup, enough to fill three and a half Olympic-size swimming pools, raced through the streets at thirty-five miles per hour, pulling buildings off their foundations. As twenty-six million pounds of molasses flooded the waterfront neighborhood, the elevated train girders on Atlantic Avenue buckled under the weight. When the sun went down, the dropping temperatures made the syrup thicker, trapping many people and horses in two feet of goo.

"The sight that greeted the first of the rescuers on the scene is almost indescribable in words. Molasses, waist deep, covered the street and swirled and bubbled about the wreckage," the *Boston Post* reported. "Here and there struggled a form—whether it was animal or human being it was impossible to tell. Only an upheaval, a thrashing about in a sticky mess, showed where any life was. Horses died like so many flies on sticky fly paper."

Twenty-one people, who ranged in ages from ten to seventy-eight, could not escape and died in the flood. Victims included Bridget Clougherty, who was crushed when the wave caused her house to collapse, and Patrick Breen, a worker who was swept into Boston Harbor. An estimated 150 people were injured and fourteen buildings were destroyed, totaling upward of $100 million in today's dollars.

The sticky mess was hard to clean up, as fresh water couldn't cut through the sludge. Fire hoses of seawater forced the molasses into the bay, staining the water brown for months. Work crews labored around the clock, eventually putting in more than eighty thousand man-hours to clear the area.

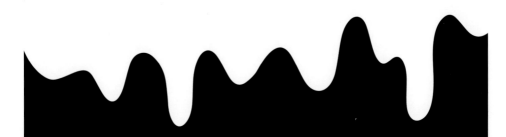

The disaster led to a lawsuit against the United States Industrial Alcohol Company. They claimed that the tank burst because of an anarchist's bomb, which weren't uncommon at the time. But after a six-year trial, they were found at fault. It was found that the steel of the holding tank was only a little more than a half inch thick, which was not strong enough to contain millions of pounds of molasses. It was also constructed by untrained workers and never reviewed by engineers and architects before it was filled. They had to pay the victims $600,000 in damages. The lawsuit changed federal laws throughout the country, so that businesses now had to hire architects and engineers for new construction and building inspectors had to sign off on projects.

It also changed the way Boston felt about molasses, which for hundreds of years has been a key ingredient in their signature baked beans. Some say that on hot days in the North End you can still smell the sweet syrup wafting through the air.

How Kimchi Led Korea into a War (of Words)

In South Korea, kimchi is part of the national identity. In a 2006 Gallup poll, Koreans placed it second only to their national flag. While many eat it daily with rice, the spicy fermented dish has been a constant for nearly three thousand years.

Koreans are serious about kimchi ... seriously. They have an annual holiday known as kimjang, when kimchi is traditionally made for the winter. There's a stock market index that tracks when Napa cabbage and the twelve other kimchi ingredients—chili, carrots, radishes, garlic, and anchovies among them—are at their best prices. When South Korea sent its first astronaut into space in 2008, kimchi went with her. There's even an entire museum, Kimchikan, in Seoul. Basically, kimchi is life.

If you're new to kimchi, you've probably tried the version made with cabbage known in Korea as *baechu*. While this is the most common type, there are hundreds of different versions using everything from daikon radish to green onion to cucumber. But what they all have in common is that the vegetables are seasoned and then placed in a closed container, often a clay pot, and fermented at a low temperature for weeks. This is where the magic happens.

But why ferment at all? The Korean diet is mainly plant-based, and fermenting helped preserve vegetables during their cold winter. Kimchi is thought to be one of the reasons Koreans have a longer life expectancy than average. In 2006, the *American Journal of Public Health* declared kimchi as one of the world's healthiest foods, scientifically proven to have multiple health benefits, as well as being an excellent source of fiber, vitamins, minerals, and antioxidants and rich in lactic acid bacteria.

Even countries that had a contentious history with Korea grew to love kimchi, including Japan. In the 1990s, they manufactured and exported a blander version using the kimchi name. Koreans were furious—it isn't even fermented! And this product came from a country that once colonized Korea and looked down on its citizens as "garlic eaters," one of the key ingredients in kimchi. Japan responded that kimchi—like tacos or curry—can be whatever a culture deems it to be. This outrage led the government of South Korea to petition the World Health Organization and the United Nations' Food and Agriculture Organization's Codex Alimentarius to set an international standard, which they did.

A similar war of words erupted in 2020, when an article in China claimed that kimchi evolved from their pickled vegetable dish, *pao cai*. South Korean food scholars went on the offensive, making the point that kimchi is fermented differently and contains fish. Plus their dish has been part of their culture for nearly three thousand years. After some spicy back-and-forth, China claimed that the article had made an error in translation and backed away from the claim. Korea allowed them to live, but they got their point across: let it be known to the world that kimchi is Korean territory, for life.

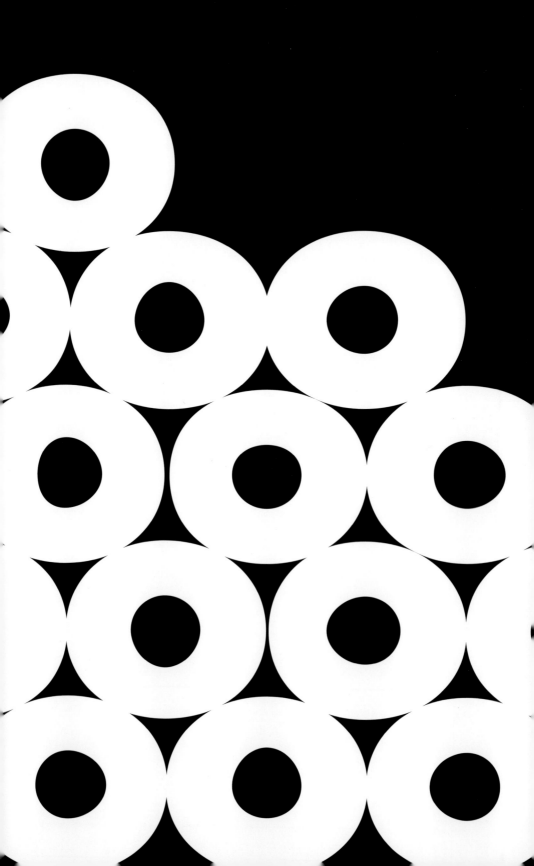

History That's
Not on the
Pop Quiz

Absolutely Not, Says Black Woman to Authorities in 1600

In 1600, a young, unmarried, mixed-race woman named Isabel de Olvera presented herself before the mayor and demanded her spot as an explorer in an expedition traveling to New Mexico.

A free woman of African descent, de Olvera lived in Querétaro, Mexico, where it was public knowledge that she was not the property of any man or woman. But in 1600, she bravely decided that she would join the Juan Guerra de Resa expedition to Santa Fe, intended to strengthen the Spanish claim to the colonized province of Santa Fe de Nuevo México. It's not known why she chose to join the expedition, although some evidence suggests that she may have been hoping to help families that had recently settled in the province. What is known is that she went willingly and not quietly into the adventure.

Knowing she could face violence and even enslavement and trafficking at her destination, de Olvera presented herself before the mayor of Querétaro, don Pedro Lorenzo de Castilla of Querétaro, and demanded an affidavit affirming her status as a free, unmarried woman. She stated:

> I am going on the expedition to New Mexico and have some reason to fear that I may be annoyed by some individual since I am a mulatta, and it is proper to protect my rights in such an eventuality by an affidavit showing that I am a free woman, unmarried and the legitimate daughter of Hernando, a Negro, and an Indian

named Magdalena. . . . I therefore request your grace to accept this affidavit, which shows that I am free and not bound by marriage or slavery. I request that a properly certified and signed copy be given to me in order to protect my rights, and that it carry full legal authority. I demand justice.

She dictated this deposition before three witnesses: Mateo Laines, a free Black man living in Querétaro; Anna Verdugo, a mestiza woman who lived near the city; and Santa Maria, a Black woman enslaved by the mayor. These witnesses offered sworn testimony affirming that she was both free and worthy, and after an eight-month legal process, de Olvera was authorized to join the expedition.

We are personally imagining her packing her bags with a flounce of determination and holding her chin up across every one of the 1,400 miles to New Mexico, as she crossed rivers, deserts, and mountain ranges, likely on foot. Little else is known about de Olvera, but she is recognized as one of the first Black women in North America to be recorded firmly demanding justice.

And she got it.

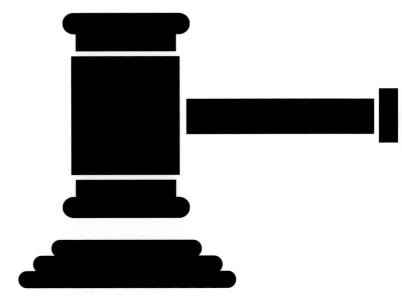

Oops, I Made a Super Useful Invention Again

We've all heard the saying "Necessity is the mother of invention," but sometimes another parent is involved, called "dumb luck." Penicillin (aka the antibiotic that has casually saved about two hundred million lives since the 1920s) is one of the most famous examples of fluke discoveries that modernize human lives. Need more proof that Lady Luck has been secretly on our side since the beginning? Then keep reading to learn about another three times humans *technically* failed but actually made something amazing.

1.

The sugar replacement Sweet'N Low was "invented" in 1878 by a man who worked with coal tar, which is a liquid byproduct of coal processing. Story has it that, after handling the substance, he ate a roll with his unwashed, *coal-tar-covered hands* and noticed an unexpected sweetness. We do know that he went on to patent the compound in 1884, but did he ever discover handwashing? That remains a mystery.

2.

According to the Andean people, the indigenous people of the Andes mountains, a key compound used to treat malaria was discovered by a feverish South American man who happened to drink water at the base of a cinchona tree. Totally parched, the man continued to drink despite the water's weird bitterness and was miraculously cured. As it turns out, the cinchona tree's bark contains quinine, an antimalarial compound that kills the parasites responsible for causing the sickness. The compound had seeped into the water from the tree and basically made a souped-up, antimalarial super tea.

3.

Ironically, dynamite was the destructive brainchild of Alfred Nobel, as in the founder of the Nobel Prize for extraordinary acts of humanitarian service. Well, technically, nitroglycerin (aka the stuff that makes dynamite go BOOM!) was unintentionally discovered by Italian chemist Ascanio Sobrero, but it was too volatile to actually use. It was Nobel who stabilized the compound and had dollar signs for eyes. He saw Sobrero's invention as an explosive source of potential wealth and ended up becoming fabulously (and ironically) wealthy after selling the patent for a weapon that revolutionized human destruction.

History's Classiest and Fiercest Burns

Almost everyone has left a cheeky reply in the comments section, but it takes a real scholar of sass to craft a clapback so epic that it even made historians say, "Write that down!" So, for all of our quick-quip queens and wisecrack-warriors, whip out those pencils and prep your notebooks because these three iconic comebacks are a master class in clapback carnage.

> **"**If I had two heads, one should be at the King of England's disposal.**"**

—**Christina of Denmark**, in a sharp pass on a marriage proposal from King Henry VIII, who had beheaded his second wife, Anne Boleyn. Christina was sixteen, and the king was thirty.

" Sir, I also heard it said that you are a wicked man. And if you are so wicked as people say, you will never get to heaven, unless you amend while you are here. **"**

—**Margery Kempe**, a woman accused of being a heretic, to the archbishop of York, the second most powerful religious figure in medieval England. She defended his accusations point by point until, in frustration, he paid a man five shillings to escort her from the room. Later, he declared that he could find no fault with her faith and wrote her a letter affirming that she was not a heretic so she could travel solo.

" If you want anything *said*, ask a man. If you want anything *done*, ask a woman. **"**

—**Margaret Thatcher**, the first female prime minister of the United Kingdom

How High Heels Kicked Gendered Fashion Standards

From the Qing Dynasty to Paris Fashion Week to your mysteriously rich aunt's walk-in closet, high heels have ruled the roost as a symbol of status, wealth, and power for centuries. In fact, historians have found evidence of platform shoes dating back to the ancient Egyptians. Not just for the wealthy, elevated shoes were also worn by butchers for the practical purpose of avoiding animal blood and entrails, yum! But what we would recognize as a true high heel wasn't invented until the 1600s by the Persians, specifically Persian men.

That's right: high heels, usually thought of as related to womanhood, were originally designed for short kings to clip them into stirrups while riding horses and to boost their height overall. Persian royalty eventually brought the high heel with them to visit France's royal court during the seventeenth century. It was here that the fancy footwear would get its foot in the door of Parisian high fashion and spread across Europe. King Louis XIV of France loved heels so much that he decreed that no one's heels could be higher than his and that red heels were strictly reserved for members of the royal family.

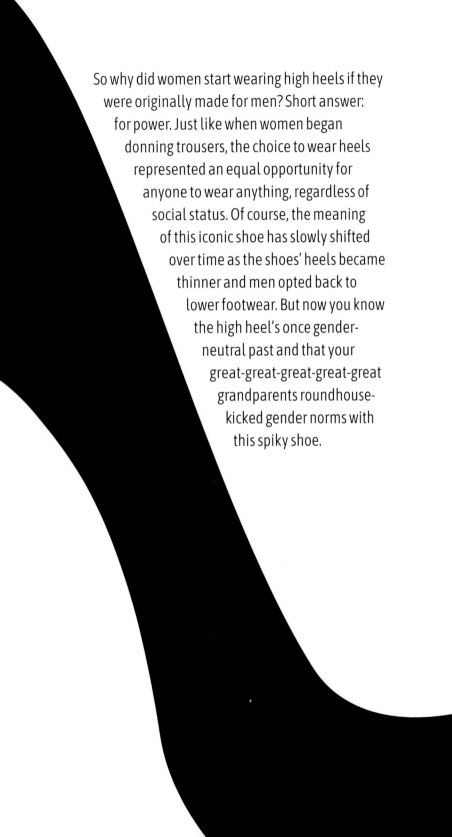

So why did women start wearing high heels if they were originally made for men? Short answer: for power. Just like when women began donning trousers, the choice to wear heels represented an equal opportunity for anyone to wear anything, regardless of social status. Of course, the meaning of this iconic shoe has slowly shifted over time as the shoes' heels became thinner and men opted back to lower footwear. But now you know the high heel's once gender-neutral past and that your great-great-great-great-great grandparents roundhouse-kicked gender norms with this spiky shoe.

The Head-Scratching Case of Olmec's Colossal Faces

Imagine this: It's the late 1850s and you're a farmer in southern Veracruz, Mexico. You've decided to clear some of the surrounding forest to make room for crops when you hit something tough, like a large boulder. You start brushing the dirt away … and then some more … and then even more, until your unplanned treasure hunt comes to a head, literally!

As it turns out, what you unearthed is the first of seventeen curious craniums that are now known as the Olmec Colossal Heads. Ranging from 3.8 to 11.2 feet (or 1.17 to 3.4 meters), these huge artifacts are stylized sculptures of human heads carved from basalt boulders and are believed to be 3D representations of people from the ancient Olmec civilization. But who are these people, why are these sculptures here in the first place, and how old are they?

Well, the answers to those questions have become a colossal mystery and a major headache for head researchers everywhere. This is because specialists haven't found written records from the Olmec, which means that a lot of speculation about the heads does not have much of a leg to stand on. Most agree that the Olmec were a sophisticated civilization with advanced technology and wide-reaching trade connections that made it possible for them to drag six- to fifty-ton blocks of basalt from thirty miles away to make their jumbo statues of important leaders. But while we are pretty confident that all of these statues come from this specific group, archaeologists debate over the artifacts' ages, which probably date back between 1400 and 1000 BCE. However we choose to wrap our minds around the Olmec sculptures, there's no denying that they were a big deal and a-head of their time.

The Art of the Fan: A Victorian's Guide to Flirting

Spanning the sixty-three years of Queen Victoria's rule over Great Britain, the Victorian era is known for its rapid industrialization, passion for ornate (sometimes deadly) fashion trends, and strict standards for personal conduct. The Victorians' obsession with propriety (or, more importantly, the *lack* of it) may have stilted their mannerisms but definitely didn't curb their desire for swoony romance (see Charlotte Brontë's *Jane Eyre* for 372 pages of evidence). Love-hungry socialites of all classes came up with some pretty creative ways to sneakily send flirtatious messages in plain sight, and no tool was better at fanning the flames of love than the hand fan.

A beautiful silk fan was a must for any lady attending a ball. It kept ladies cool and could signal a bachelorette's amorous intentions when carried according to "the fan code." Partially a promotional gimmick, shops would sell fans and print pamphlets that explained the meaning behind how someone was using their accessory. For example, carrying an open fan in one's left hand meant "speak with me" while quick fluttering signaled that they were already engaged. Other codes included placing the handle on the lips as an invitation for a kiss, twirling it in the right hand to show that their heart belonged to another, and worst of all, dropping the fan to place a suiter into the friend zone—ouch. Even though the art of the fan may seem antiquated by our modern standards, the fan code gave women a rare opportunity to make the first move and make their desires known.

Three More Ways the Victorians Put the "Rizz" in Charisma

1. **Photo collages:** Photography was new and trendy during this time, so lovebirds used photo collages as an opportunity to show their love interest their creative side. After all, nothing screams "hip, single, and ready to mingle" like pasting a photo of a lady on the back of a giant flamingo, right?

2. **Classified ads:** Popular way before the song "Escape," Victorians would put their romantic passions on public display in their local newspapers. They invented pen names and wrote impassioned notes like, "KITTEN, I hope you are happy. I am most miserable. Do write to our house before Wednesday next; I cannot bear a year. Pray let me see you for old love, which is still stronger."

3. **Passionate letters:** Before we could slide into someone's DMs, sending a letter was one of the most direct (and only) ways to contact a potential partner. Of course, respectable correspondence requires a strict code of conduct. Eager scribes would buy letter-writing manuals with posh-approved letter templates during this time.

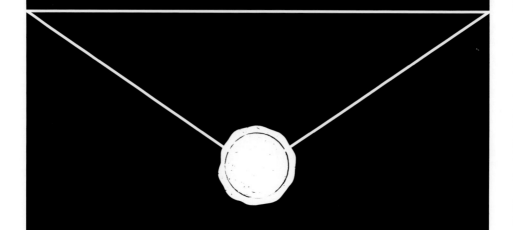

The Self-Taught Scholar Who Called Out Thomas Jefferson

When Thomas Jefferson wrote "All men are created equal," he didn't mean Black people. He enslaved more than six hundred people during his lifetime, including his own children, coercively conceived with his slave Sally Hemings. He wrote that they were inferior to whites and "as incapable as children."

This is the world Benjamin Banneker was born into in 1731 as a free Black man in rural Maryland. Unlike many of his fellow citizens, he learned how to read and write and was taught for a few years at a one-room schoolhouse.

An autodidact, Banneker was curious about the world and what made it tick. In an early show of his budding genius, Banneker borrowed a pocket watch, studied how it worked, and then built a wooden clock that kept perfect time for decades. Some claim it was one of the first clocks built in America.

Banneker was a hardcore nerd, teaching himself advanced mathematics, as well as how to play the flute and violin, all of which he did when he wasn't running his one-hundred-acre tobacco farm. In his later years, he befriended the Ellicotts, a Quaker family who moved to the area from Pennsylvania. George Ellicott was a land surveyor with an interest in astronomy. Banneker had recently retired from farming at age fifty-eight, so he started studying Ellicott's technical books and lunar tables. Before long, he correctly forecasted an eclipse, which other learned astronomers had gotten wrong.

Meanwhile, Ellicott's brother, Andrew, was hired as an engineer to help oversee the building of the new federal city: Washington, DC. He needed a hand, so he hired Banneker as an assistant surveyor. His work was called out in 1791 by the *Georgetown Weekly Ledger*, which wrote, "[Ellicott] is attended by Benjamin Banniker, an Ethiopian, whose abilities, as a surveyor, and an astronomer, clearly prove that Mr. Jefferson's concluding that race of men were void of mental endowments, was without foundation."

After finishing the surveying and witnessing the installation of the four stone markers that delineated the corners of the Federal District, Banneker returned to his farm. There he wrote his first almanac, filled with information about the cosmos and other words of wisdom. A fellow scientist reviewed the work, writing that the almanac was "a very extraordinary performance, considering the colour of the Author." Banneker was irritated, writing, "I am annoyed to find that the subject of my race is so much stressed. The work is either correct or it is not. In this case, I believe it to be perfect."

This frustration may have led Banneker to send a handwritten copy of his almanac to Thomas Jefferson. In the accompanying letter, he called out Jefferson for his quest for liberty for the colonies but at the same time imposing slavery on Banneker's people. He wrote, "In detaining by fraud and violence so numerous a part of my brethren, under groaning captivity and cruel oppression, that you should at the same time be found guilty of that most criminal act, which you professedly detested in others."

Jefferson responded that he understood the paradox and said he found the institution reprehensible. Like many slave owners at the time, he profited too heavily from the institution to truly work to outlaw it and never planned to free anyone.

Undeterred, Banneker published the correspondence, which went through multiple printings. While he didn't write more about Jefferson, Banneker continued to spotlight his genius in his "perfect" almanac, which he published for years with his picture prominently on the cover.

Stonehenge! Going Once, Going Twice! SOLD!

What's one thing you and Cecil Chubb have in common? No, it's not piña coladas or getting caught in the rain (unfortunately). Chubb was a bargain hunter with an eye for good deals. It was this thrifty impulse that threw off the course of Cecil's shopping plans on a brisk September afternoon in 1915. Originally instructed to buy a set of reasonably priced dining chairs at the local auction, the lawyer completely forgot the assignment when the auctioneer opened bidding for the deal of a lifetime: "Stonehenge with about thirty acres, two rods, thirty-seven perches of adjoining downland." And that's how Cecil walked away with a world heritage site for the low, low cost of £6,600, which is about $1 million by today's standards (what a deal!).

But you're probably wondering: how could a priceless prehistoric monument possibly end up on the auction block in the first place? The short answer is pretty simple: estate sale. It turns out that Stonehenge has a long and complicated history of ownership. Before being turned over to the British government, the monument had been privately owned by the local Benedictine abbey, King Henry VIII, and several wealthy British families, like the Antrobus estate. The deed to Stonehenge eventually became a part of Sir Edmund Antrobus's extensive estate and holdings. The neolith then went to auction shortly after Sir Antrobus's death, which is where our fellow bargain hunter, Cecil, comes in. Living only three miles from the site in Salisbury, England, Cecil told local newspapers pretty matter-of-factly, "While I was in the [auction] room, I thought a Salisbury man ought to buy it, and that is how it was done."

Despite his earnest-seeming motivations, his partner, Mary Chubb, was not as thrilled about his monumental purchase. Fast-forward to 1918 and Cecil gifted Stonehenge to the British government with little ado. In his letter about the donation, he wrote, "I became the owner of it with a deep sense of pleasure, and had contemplated that it might remain a cherished possession of my family for long years to come. It has, however, been pressed upon me that the nation would like to have it for its own, and would prize it most highly." And that's how Stonehenge was purchased and then returned. As for the sensibly priced chairs, we sadly have no closure on that part of the story.

Three More Auction Block-Busters

- **A piece of scrap paper from Albert Einstein:** Einstein was staying in a Tokyo hotel when he learned he won the Nobel Prize. Excited, he hastily wrote on the nearest scrap of paper, "A calm and modest life brings more happiness than the pursuit of success combined with constant restlessness." And that's the note that eventually went for $1.56 million at auction in 2017.

- **A lobster-shaped rotary phone:** Sprung from the mind of Salvador Dalí, a white rotary phone with matching white lobster receiver was sold for $1.058 million, and that's without Bluetooth.

- **A cake fit for a king:** A singular slice of cake from Prince Charles and Princess Diana's wedding in 1981 sold for a whopping £1,850 (or $2,321) and showed the world just how much it costs to own a slice of history.

The Impossible Mummification of Xin Zhui

Xin Zhui is famous for her supple skin, long eyelashes, and silken locks. She's also been dead for over 2,200 years. That's right— you're probably feeling just as baffled and amazed as the team of archeologists who discovered this almost perfectly preserved body in 1971.

Uncovered in Hunan, China, Xin Zhui, also known as Lady Dai, was found alongside 1,400 other artifacts (read: she was a *very* wealthy woman). And while her tomb and belongings have taught us a lot about life around 200 BCE, it's her shockingly lifelike remains that really astonish researchers. Not only does she still have a dewy complexion, but upon discovery her mummy still had food in the stomach, identifiable fingerprints, and liquid blood in her veins (she had Type A blood, for anyone who's curious). In other words, her skin care game puts our ten-step routines to shame.

Scientists still don't really know how people pulled off such a perfect preservation, but they have a few clues. First, the body was obviously prepared very carefully before burial and cleaned of anything that might accelerate decomposition. Second, she was placed into a Russian dolls' nest of airtight coffins. Finally, the layered coffin was buried deep underground and packed with a combination of charcoal and white clay. This final step ensured that the mummified body was kept cool, dry, and safely sealed, at least for a couple millennia.

Three Delights from Lady Dai's Digs

1. A T-shaped silk banner was found in the innermost of Xin Zhui's four coffins. Over six feet long, the silk was hand-painted and depicts the lady's funeral and ascent into the heavenly realm.

2. Just like the Egyptians would have done, Lady Dai's attendants made sure she had everything she could possibly need in the afterlife, like a wardrobe of one hundred silk outfits.

3. She was also sent with 182 dishes, which would be more than enough for her and the 162 wooden figurines that represented her waitstaff in the great beyond.

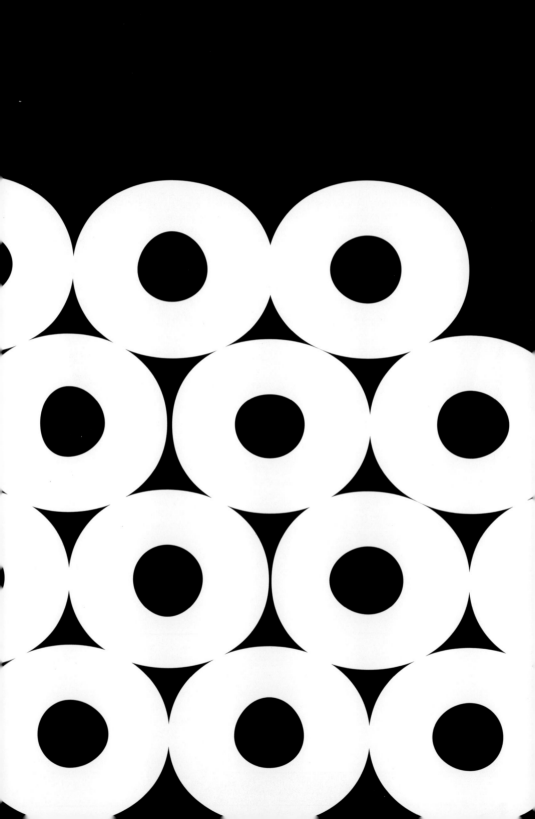

5

Language We Want
a Few Words With

Vintage Slang
That Will Never
Be Outdated

Every generation invents new slang, but some are more "creative"
than others. These are a few retro words that are delightfully useful
and weird and deserve a mainstream revival. Toss one out at your
next holiday dinner and see who's in the know and who doesn't know
their onions.

Flub the dub (v.): to evade a duty or obligation

Ralph would do anything to get out of the mile run in gym, so he's sprained his ankle yesterday just to *flub the dub*.

The cat's pajamas (adj.): the best of the best

The McDonald's on Second Street is *the cat's pajamas*. It has a ball pit and a working ice cream machine.

Pang-wangle (v.): to continue living cheerfully
in spite of minor inconveniences

Despite the gloomy weather, poor Wi-Fi signal, and incorrect coffee order, Cecile *pang-wangled* through it all with her perpetually sunny optimism.

Know your onions (v.): to be aware of what's up

Eloise, you've got to unmute the group chat, or you'll never get the tea and *know your onions*!

A butter and egg man (n.): a rich but naive country boy
who acts like a Casanova when he's in the big city

Did you hear that Louis sold the family farm to a pickleball court developer and moved to the city? Now he thinks that he's a real big shot, but he still wears jeans to Michelin Star restaurants like the *butter and egg man* he is.

Five Weirdly Long Palindromes for the Ambidextrous Reader

Technically speaking, palindromes can be any text or numerical sequence that reads the same forward as it does backward, like the word "kayak," the number 180081, or even the date December 2, 2021. This simple requirement means that palindromes can be ridiculously long but also total nonsense. In fact, one of the world's longest palindromic phrases is a seemingly random list of 21,012 words (also a palindromic number) that was generated by a computer program!

Although most of us probably don't have the time (or stamina) to recite a 21,012-word sentence, there are several single-word palindromes that are also pretty impressive. Here are some of the longest known palindromes that you can (probably) work into a conversation:

1.
Rotavator

A device that tills soil with rotating blades. This machine was invented by Arthur Clifford Howard around World War I and revolutionized farming. By combining rotating hoes with an internal combustion engine, Howard automated the tilling process and truly turned over a new leaf for agriculture everywhere.

2.
Tattarrattat

The sound of someone knocking on a door. The word first appeared in James Joyce's 1922 novel *Ulysses* and earns bonus points for doubling as an onomatopoeia.

3.
Malayalam

The language of the Malayali people. One of the six classical languages of India, Malayalam is spoken by over thirty million people, which is almost equivalent to the population of Texas.

4.
Detartrated

The removal of tartrates from liquid. A tartrate is a type of salt usually found in juice or wine that causes a sour or tart taste. Detartration not only makes things sweeter but also creates the byproduct potassium bitartrate, aka cream of tartar.

5.
Saippuakivikauppias

The Finnish term for "soapstone vendor." We applaud anyone who can casually bring up this word in their everyday conversation AND ballpark a correct pronunciation at the same time.

Two Words to Zap Everyone Awake

Lazy day? A loquacious word might be just the lightning bolt you need to look alive again. Yes, it won't make your work or your laundry go away. But it will make you giggle like a lunatic to yourself, and it will deter anyone from talking to you, like, ever. And that's a win in our book. So toss out these two words to let others know just how terrific a hippopotomonstrosesquipedalian word (a very, very long word) can be at adding some spice to those snooze-y day vibes.

1.
Floccinaucinihilipilification

The longest word in the *Oxford English Dictionary*. It means "the action or habit of estimating as worthless."

"Every Wednesday people hit me with their floccinaucinihilipilification about hump day, but that's just because they haven't tried out logomaniacal logo-diarrhea as an antidote to listlessness."

2.

Lopadotemachoselachogaleokranioleipsanodrimhypo-trimmatosilphioparaomelitokatakechymenokichlepikos-syphophattoperisteralektryonoptekephalliokigklopeleio-lagoiosiraiobaphetraganopterygon

The longest literary word and the longest culinary word. It's the English transliteration of a Greek word coined by Aristophanes in his play *The Ecclesiazusae*. It means "a hash made from leftover food accumulated over two weeks." The Greek lists all seventeen ingredients.

"What's for dinner?" "Lopadotemachoselachoga…" Keep going until they walk away.

The Birth of the "Antarctic Accent"

Where do accents come from? The answer to this simple question seems pretty obvious: distinct accents develop in groups of people who are isolated together for a significant amount of time. But although linguists understand this in theory, no one has had the chance to study the development of a new one because recording technology needed to track these slight changes in speech is—you guessed it—a relatively new invention. At least, this was the case until a curious case study appeared very recently.

Antarctica is one of the most inhospitable places on Earth and unsurprisingly has no native human population. People didn't set foot on the continent until 1821, and even the accuracy of that date is hotly debated! It's only because of technological advancements and an international effort that a small group of people have been able to set up temporary shop in recent times.

Mostly made up of scientists and support staff, the human population of Antarctica peaks at around five thousand in the summer but then plunges to a meager one thousand people, creatively called "winterers." What attracted researchers from the University of Munich to this cold cohort was their linguistic diversity (i.e., people with different native accents) and their extreme isolation during the harsh winter months. The linguists tracked eleven winterers and recorded them saying a list of words before, during, and after their isolation period. By the end of the study, they saw a convergence of once-distinct accents into something more uniformed and unique from the subjects' original speech. So, next time you hear an accent you can't quite place, try guessing the newly minted Antarctic accent!

Three More Reasons the South Pole Is Weird

Ironically, Antarctica is the driest place on Earth but also holds most of its fresh water (about 70 percent) as ice.

Antarctica is protected under its own treaty. Since history has the habit of repeating itself, the discovery of an unpopulated continent sparked *a lot* of tensions between countries. Things were settled peacefully in 1959 when twelve countries signed the Antarctic Treaty, which agreed to preserve the continent for research purposes. We love effective diplomacy.

It's technically a desert, just a cold one! That's because a desert is any place that gets very little rain, and with an annual average of 0.4 inches (10 millimeters) of rainfall a year, Antarctica fits the bill.

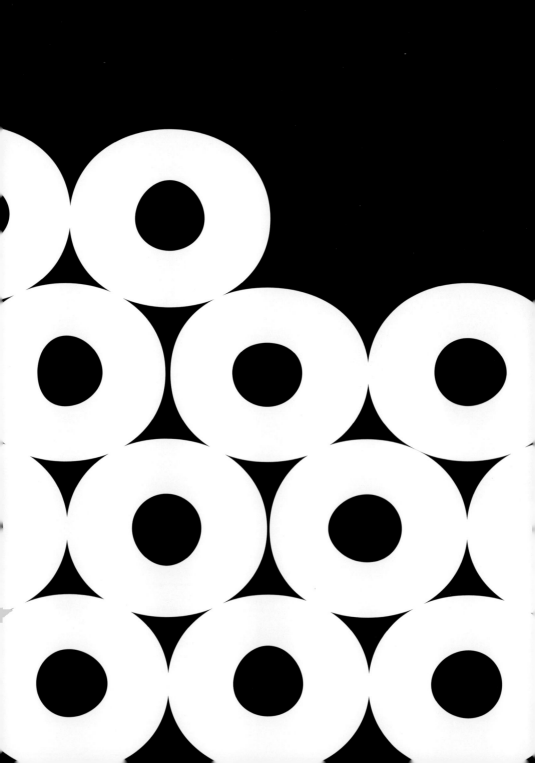

6

Science Stories with Explosive Results

Five Ways Human Bodies Are Kind of Meta

Have you ever thought about how you are inside of yourself...at all times? And how your brain is actually part of your body, not just a floating orb shouting commands down to a sometimes cooperative meat sack? If the body blows your mind, then snuggle up close to these pretty freaky facts about this lump of bones and flesh we haul around.

1.

When you blush, the lining of your stomach also turns red.

2.

Teratomas are a kind of tumor that can grow their own teeth and hair.

3.

The human body glows in the dark, but the glow is too faint for the human eye to detect.

4.

The ovaries of a baby contain all the eggs they will ever have. So, on a cellular level, you already existed inside your mother when she was inside your grandmother, like a Russian nesting doll.

5.

If facing extreme starvation, it's possible your brain would begin to eat itself.

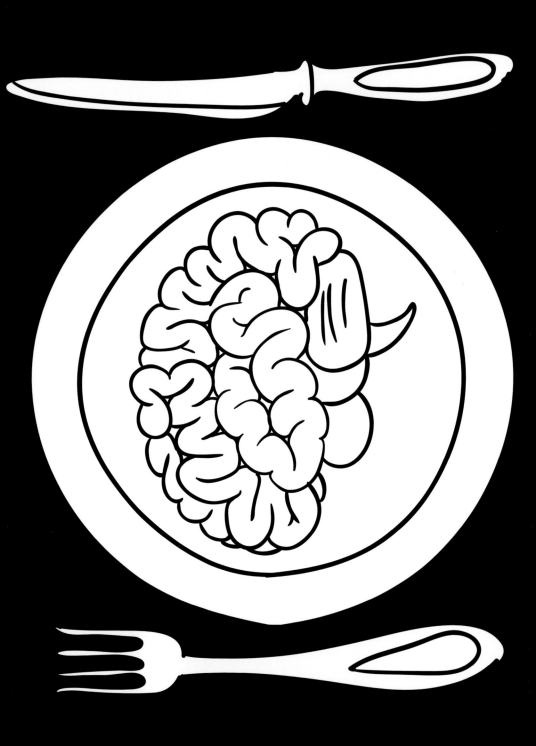

But How Big Is One Billion? Nine Ways to Imagine Nine Zeros

What do American fashion designer Ralph Lauren, Walmart heiress Alice Walton, and Swedish businessman Stefan Persson all have in common? You guessed it, they're all Libras...AND billionaires. In fact, according to one study, Libra is the most common star sign for billionaires!

But while a lot of people can paint a pretty accurate picture of a stereotypical Libra (indecisiveness and all), how many of us could actually describe what a billion looks like? Here are nine ways to bring this mind-blowing number into perspective:

1.

If you saved $100 per day, you would become a billionaire in a short 27,397 years. If you did it in fifty years, then you would need to put away $1.6 million per month or a cool $54,700 *per day*.

2.

Counting to a billion requires at least 95.1 years of nonstop speaking. This calculation makes the generous assumption that you can say each number in around an average of three seconds, so it will take about three billion seconds to reach your goal.

3.

One billion seconds is equal to 31.69 years or 11,574 days. So, instead of wishing someone a happy thirty-first birthday, you could congratulate them on almost reaching a billion seconds!

4.

A stack of one billion $1 bills is over 343 times the official height of the Eiffel Tower, which is 984 feet or 300 meters. This equates to roughly 336,846 feet tall, which puts Mount Everest's 29,032 feet to shame.

5.

If we assume that one grain of sand is 1 mm³, then a billion grains of sand would fill a box that is 1 m³ in volume. This cubic meter of sand would weigh 1.6 tons or 3,527.4 pounds, which is heavier than the average midsize sedan.

6.

A small library typically holds anywhere between 1,000 to 3,000 books in its collection. This means that a billion books could be divided up into one million 1,000-book libraries.

7.

The distance between the earth and the moon is 238,900 miles. This means that a person would have to go between these two bodies over 4,185 times to travel one billion miles.

8.

It would take one hundred million extra-large, ten-slice pizzas to equal a billion slices of pie. The average extra-large pizza has a surface area of two hundred square inches, so one hundred million of them would be twenty billion square inches or a little less than five square miles of cheesy, cheesy deliciousness.

9.

The average roll of toilet paper is perforated into 333 squares. You need to buy 3,003,003.003 rolls for your booty to crack a billion.

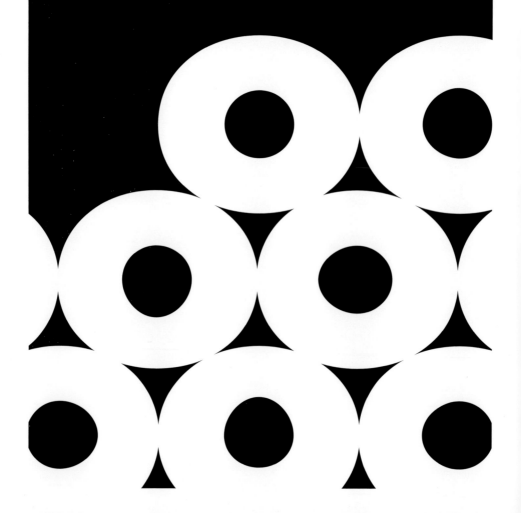

High-Tech and Low-Cost: How a Hitchhiking Robot Traveled the World for Free

Putting the "drive" in hard drive, hitchBOT was the beepin' and boopin' brainchild of two Canadian professors who wanted to answer one very important question: can robots trust humans? (You haven't asked yourself this?) To test it, the researchers designed a small, solar-powered machine with a cylindrical body, bendy limbs, and a digital screen that displayed its eyes and mouth. The robot was coded to hold basic conversations, tell fun facts, and most importantly, ask for a ride to its next destination! On top of never asking for a pitstop, hitchBOT was the ideal travel companion.

Guided by a zero-dollar travel budget and sporting an iconic pair of yellow rain boots, this robot lived out the dream of broke college students everywhere and "studied abroad" completely for free. hitchBOT successfully toured Canada, Germany, and the Netherlands thanks to its trusty car seat and the kindness of complete strangers from 2013 to 2015. It documented its adventures with posts on its social media accounts and quickly gained a worldwide web of commuters offering literal tech support for the lone explorer. Now a micro-influencer, it used its platform for good and promoted positive human-robot interactions (the free upgrades to first class and adoring followers were just a bonus!). hitchBOT believed in the goodness of people until the very end of its travels. In its final message to the world, it wrote, "My love for humans will never fade," a final goodbye that warms our motherboard and brings a tear to our interface.

Five Random Objects Sent into Space That Will Make You Ask, "Why?"

Space, the final frontier for starry-eyed adventurers, ambitious scientists, and ... treadmills named after late-night talk show hosts? No longer just for humans and a few unlucky house pets, missions into space have carried all sorts of wild and wacky things into the Milky Way, and these are some of our favorites.

1.
Cars

Tesla redefined the meaning of "all-terrain vehicle" in 2018 when they launched a red Tesla Roadster into the cosmos. Luckily, the car is fully electric, so refueling in the vacuum of space won't be a problem.

2.
Lightsabers

Luke Skywalker's lightsaber from *Star Wars: Episode VI—Return of the Jedi* (1983) found itself back among the stars in 2007 to celebrate the *Star Wars* franchise's thirtieth anniversary. It was accompanied by seven astronauts and jettisoned into the atmosphere via the force, specifically g-force.

3.
Delivery pizza

In 2001, Pizza Hut embarked on its own space odyssey and became the first company to nearly hit the moon with a big pizza pie. The delivery time took sixty days and had to rely on the Russian space agency to act as delivery person, but the pizza did make it to the International Space Station (ISS) in one piece and proved that pizza really does taste out of this world.

4.
Amelia Earhart's wristwatch

Amelia Earhart is best known for being the first woman to fly solo across the Atlantic Ocean, but she was also an organizer as well as a trailblazer. Earhart was the first president of the Ninety-Nines (an international association of licensed women pilots), which has many members, including the astronaut Shannon Walker. Walker received the watch that Earhart wore for both of her trans-Atlantic excursions. She honored Earhart's role in cracking the glass ceiling by having Earhart's memento break through our atmospheric ceiling.

5.
A treadmill named after Stephen Colbert

Harnessing the power of his adoring fans, Stephen Colbert came in first in an online vote created by NASA to decide what the name would be for a new room added to the ISS. Sadly, NASA did maintain the right to discount write-in votes and did not name the room after the comedian, BUT they did come up with a compromise. Around the same time, NASA was preparing to send a newly designed treadmill to the space station (because even without gravity, you can still run?). They ended up renaming the machine the "Combined Operational Load Bearing External Resistance Treadmill," which forms the acronym "COLBERT."

A Multidimensional Head-Scratcher: Five Puzzling Rubik's Cube Facts

Multicolored, multisided, and multi-infuriating, the Rubik's Cube is the iconic 3D puzzle that has enraged—wait, we mean *engaged*—millions of minds across the world since 1974. Although it looks like a simple game, these Rubik's Cube facts will leave your brain as twisted as that unfinished cube in your desk drawer.

1.

The puzzle was originally named the "Magic Cube." The name was shot down because the company producing the toy thought that it gave off witchcraft vibes. This sadly confirms that a *Harry Potter* x Rubik's Cube collaboration is probably not coming soon.

2.

"Speedcubing" is the competitive sport of solving a Rubik's Cube of various dimensions as quickly as possible. In 2023, the world record for the fastest time completing a 3x3 rotating cube was set by an American, Max Park, who solved the puzzle in 3.13 seconds.

3.

The first speedcubing world championship took place in Budapest in 1982. The fastest time was also set by an American, so you could say that the US has a corner on the speedcubing market.

4.

The "Masterpiece Cube" is the most expensive Rubik's Cube ever made, with an estimated value of $2.5 million. The 3x3 cube has a gold base and is coated with 1,350 precious stones.

5.

In 2003, a man solved the puzzle in 32 seconds while *falling 12,000 feet from a plane*. Next time, we're hoping to see him play chess from a 20,000-foot drop.

Warning: This Pigment May Cause Discoloration or Death

What do the color green and stomach cancer have in common? Both helped kill ex-emperor Napoleon Bonaparte deader than a Parisian snail at the dinner table. But how could Napoleon's favorite color be the key to his demise?

Specifically known as Scheele's Green, this toxic tone captured the public's hearts (and lives) during the nineteenth century with its vibrant hue. The color was created from a mixture of sodium carbonate and *arsenious* oxide, and yes, this is going exactly where you think it is.

Scheele's arsenic-laced pigment found its way into everything, and we mean *everything*. Coats, candles, gloves, wallpaper, children's toys, shoes, carpets, pants, and even food dye (fun fact: the Scottish are still suspicious of artificially green candy because of Scheele's Green). Arsenic's poisonous power was not common knowledge during this time, so swooning ladies in bright emerald dresses and sickly children in chartreuse playrooms became a standard part of the Victorian aesthetic.

The madness continued until 1861 when factory worker Matilda Scheurer became so ill from handling a powdered form of the pigment that *she turned green*. Matilda reportedly vomited green, developed green-stained eyes and nails, and lost the ability to see anything except Scheele's Green. The young girl's horrible death spotlighted the dangerous reality of the toxic pigment and gripped the public as a heartbreaking cautionary tale.

Unlike Napoleon, whose slow poisoning by his green-painted walls went unrecognized, the story of Matilda's death became a rallying cry for change. Since then, the color's popularity thankfully waned significantly, only to make a brief reappearance on the market as a pesticide until the 1930s, when it was finally removed from use completely.

Hurricane or Grandma?

Hurricanes are not what you might call comforting. First, there's the torrential rain and the wind that reaches a nonstop speed of at least seventy-four miles per hour. There's also that eerie eye-of-the-storm feeling. And the storm surges. And the all-encompassing destruction across thousands of miles. And the threat of losing your life and all you love.

Contrast that to the warm, fuzzy, sunshine-y feeling you would get when you visited your grandma and she would make you your favorite soup and call you "sugar" and "queenie."

There are some differences there? We think? As soon as you're done questioning your reality, we invite you to realize that we are all being gaslit to associate cataclysmic tropical cyclones with adorable fluffy-headed Miss Marple-ites.

Who is behind this nefarious nomenclature? The answer: the World Meteorological Organization, which is not a part of the Marvel Universe. (Yet.)

Since 1979, the WMO has kept six international name lists that are used to name precipitous precipitation. So, every six years, you might run into the same stormy characters. Luckily, someone at the WMO had at least one particle of sense to know that the names of hurricanes that were catastrophically destructive and deeply traumatic need to go on the retired-with-no-comeback-tour list.

Also showing what might actually be growth and awareness for a governmental body, the names have become increasingly reflective of the diversity in the world. But the names on the 1995–2008 list were still quite a doozy, youngster. Can you spot which ones are quaintly moniker-ed natural disasters and which ones are harmless octogenarians?

- Hortense
- Beryl
- Opal
- Hermine
- Frances
- Bertha
- Gert
- Iris
- Ophelia
- Fay
- Florence
- Dolly
- Arlene
- Nana

Answer: All of these are hurricane names. And they're probably also someone's grandparent's name. Take your appellation appeals to the bad eggs at the WMO.

Chernobyl Is Run by Mutant Mushrooms

The explosion of a reactor at the Chernobyl Nuclear Power Plant in 1986 has fascinated the world for decades and is now considered the worst nuclear accident in history. The disaster ultimately claimed the lives of at least thirty people following its immediate wake and required the evacuation of around 350,000 people. Massive cleanup efforts that targeted nuclear waste took place over the next seven months, but the area was soon abandoned out of safety concerns.

With human activity gone, other life in Chernobyl has taken over. Some plants have thrived just because they've been given the chance to grow uninterrupted, but other organisms have spread like wildfire because of the lingering radioactivity itself. Take *Cryptococcus neoformans*, a species of radiotrophic mushroom that has claimed squatters' rights in Chernobyl and provided an invaluable service in exchange: absorbing the site's excess radiation.

Radiotrophic fungi are a type of shroom that can "eat" radiation and convert it into energy for itself. They're able to do this because they have very high levels of melanin, aka the same pigment that we have in our skin, included within their mycelium (their root system). Just like humans after a long day in the sun, radiotrophic mycelia use their melanin to convert radiation into energy through a process called radiosynthesis, which is like photosynthesis! So, although Chernobyl is still too radioactive for humans, we know that our return could be in the cards thanks to these hungry and hardworking fungi.

More Fun(gus) Facts

- Mushrooms are more closely related to humans than plants. Although technically neither, members of the fungi kingdom share more similarities with the animal kingdom, like "breathing" oxygen and feeding themselves with organic materials rather than through photosynthesis.

- As of 2018, the iconic duo known as flora and fauna welcomed a third category of organisms into their tight friend group: funga! Now, the flora, fauna, and funga trio refer to many more diverse levels of life that range from mammal to mycelium.

- The largest living organism ever discovered is a mushroom. In 1998, people stumbled upon 2,384 acres (nearly 10 square kilometers) covered by a honey mushroom in Oregon. Even crazier, scientists believe that the shroom could be over 8,000 years old!

- Some mushrooms can make their own wind. Recent studies from Harvard have observed that some mushrooms can generate a breeze strong enough to lift themselves several inches off the ground and move laterally. Researchers theorize that this ability probably helps the mushrooms spread their spores.

How the Shannon Number Has More Digits Than Stars in the Universe

In 1948, American mathematician and computer scientist Claude Shannon asked a deceptively simple question: which value is greater, the number of atoms in the universe or the number of possible chess moves? Although people had speculated that chess might have an infinite number of possible games, no one had tried to quantify that number exactly until Shannon decided to take on this potentially impossible task in 1950. Basically, he wanted to figure out whether a computer could calculate enough of those possibilities to beat human players at the game of kings (this landmark defeat would eventually happen twenty years later). And what he found was big: as in more-possible-games-than-atoms-in-the-observable-universe big.

Scientists say that there are somewhere between 10^{78} and 10^{82} atoms in all of the universe that we can see, thanks to modern technology, which is a lot. To spell that estimation out, that's a range spanning from ten quadrillion vigintillion to one hundred thousand quadrillion vigintillion atoms (try saying that five times fast). But how does this compare to the Shannon Number? If we exclude all illegal moves, then the value is a measly 10^{40} moves, but Shannon wanted to know

every possible option and decided to include banned plays. Just by incorporating about thirty more moves, his calculation shot up to 10^{120} positions. After coming up with this number, he concluded that a computer calculating every chess combination wasn't a realistic concern because it would take the computer more time than the current age of the universe to generate every possibility. In other words, we know what assignment to give computers to stall an AI takeover of the world for a *looooooooong* time.

Chess Trivia Sure to Impress—Rook, Line, and Sinker

1. In 1989, the longest official game of chess went on for twenty hours and took 269 moves to finish.

2. In theory, it is possible to checkmate someone in just two moves.

3. Chess experts estimate that there are over 168 octillion possible ways to play just the first ten moves of a game. To put that in perspective, a singular octillion is the number 1 followed by not eight but *twenty-seven zeros.*

4. The rule that lets a pawn move two spaces on the player's first move was invented by the Spanish in 1280.

5. The folding chessboard was invented by a priest who was told to stop playing chess. They created the foldable board to better hide in between books.

The Belly Button Biodiversity Project, or Navel-Gazing for Science

Look at your belly button. Do you see anything special? The answer is probably "no" unless you have wicked lint action going on. In most cases, there's really no reason to give a belly button more than a passing glance, but the scientists of the Belly Button Biodiversity Project dared to look deeper and found something truly amazing.

Launched in 2011 by North Carolina State University (NC State), this large-scale project homed in on a small-scale microbiome, meaning the human navel. Technically called *umbilicus*, our belly buttons are unique from other mammals because they're a relatively big scar compared to the flat divots or small slits of our fur-covered cousins. That makes the human navel a marvelous oddity and a marvelous home for tiny creatures. And when we say "tiny," we mean literally microscopic. In partnership with the North Carolina Museum of Natural Sciences, biologists at NC State were interested in teaching people more about the microscopic organisms that live in your belly button rent free.

The project's ongoing goal is to spread the word that all body bacteria isn't bad bacteria by identifying the creatures that live in your navel, at least when they actually know what they are. Of the 66 samples collected in their first set of volunteers, researchers found 2,368 different species of microorganisms, and more than half of them had never been discovered before! They also noticed that each person was home to about 67 different species but that very few people had ones in common. In fact, only 8 of the 2,368 microorganisms were found in at least 70 percent of test subjects. Ultimately, it's more proof that you and your little army of tiny creatures are truly one of a kind.

Digging Deeper into Some Navel Nonsense

- Women's navels were banned from American television during the 1960s, but this censorship was luckily dismissed before any Free the Belly Button campaigns got traction.

- The lint in your belly button and in your dryer actually have a lot in common because both come from your clothing.

- The fancy word for "navel-gazing" is "omphaloskepsis." *Merriam-Webster* defines this word as "contemplation of one's navel as an aid to meditation," for all you belly button Buddhas out there.

Introducing the Neutrino, the Universe's Strangest Particle

If we remember anything from high school science courses, it's two things: 1) mitochondria are the powerhouse of the cell, and 2) energy cannot be created or destroyed (aka the law of conservation of energy). These basic rules of biology and physics are foundational to how we make sense of the world. So that's why scientists get clammy hands when those rules start looking not-so-true.

Enter the neutrino. The neutrino particle was first hypothesized to exist in the 1930s because of a blip in the law of conservation of energy. At the time, scientists noticed that some energy was going missing while studying the decay of a beta particle. This radically unexpected change needed an explanation, and that explanation was a nearly imperceptible subatomic particle named the neutrino. Kind of like the electron's ghostly cousins, neutrinos are particles with very little to no mass, no charge, and weak nuclear force. They are also one of the most abundant particles in the universe but ironically one of the most difficult ones to detect as well. Case in point, the Sudbury Neutrino Observatory has a thousand-ton machine designed just to search for these illusive specks. The machine can theoretically detect up to 1,012 neutrinos per second, but what does it pick up on in reality? Thirty. As in, only *thirty neutrinos a day*.

So, why are researchers so invested in something that barely exists? Mostly because it's a byproduct of nuclear fusion, which means that the future of neutrino research is very bright! So, to these scientists, more power to you. No, really, we're sure your electric bill must be through the roof.

Three More Reasons Neutrinos Are a Serious Matter

1. Instead of bumping into matter, neutrinos kind of just zip *through* stuff, including us! It's estimated that about one hundred trillion neutrinos pass through us every second.

2. Just like the contents of a glitter bomb, neutrinos from the Big Bang cover the entire universe and make their way into everything, which is why you carry about fifteen million of these particles in your body and roughly three hundred of them in one pinky finger alone!

3. Neutrinos are harmless ... for now. Maybe from reading a little too much sci-fi, some scientists think that they could create a neutrino beam. Luckily for us, they'd have to find some neutrinos first.

You Could Hold a Black Hole in Your Hand

Yes, that's right. Imagine, a black hole gently cupped in your hands any time you want. That's because a black hole is not a literal hole. It's a thing, with mass and density, just like a coffee cup. And theoretically, black holes could exist that are so small you could snuggle them into the palm of your hand.

A black hole is basically a massive ton of mass. But it's still an object, just one that's extremely dense, like a million Earths packed into your mailbox. This also gives it extreme gravity, even if it's relatively small. According to NASA, black holes can be any size, even as small as an atom. So, if you came upon a black hole that was the size of the period at the end of this sentence, you could, in theory, pick it up and pocket it for later.

The only thing that would really stop you is that it would weigh as much as a mountain. And the gravitational pull would begin to "spaghettify" you, stretching you out into a long, thin shape as it pulled you closer. And then you would die.

But let's say you could, in theory, exist in your human body inside of a black hole. What would it be like? For starters, there would be no "here" and no "now." It's believed that time and space don't exist inside of black holes. There would be no distance between, say, your hand and your shoulder, and there would be no time to wonder, "How long have I been inside this black hole?" because time wouldn't exist. You would exist in a way that is utterly incomprehensible to our human brains. You would also never, ever be able to escape. But, silver lining—

you would have escaped from the inescapable: death and taxes! Well, except for the death part. Just taxes.

Depressing, yes. But on the bright side, black holes don't really suck up anything and everything around them. They're actually quite selective in what they shred for eternity.

For instance, you could hop into the Tesla Roadster currently orbiting the earth and park outside a black hole and be fine until the end of time. You'd feel the gravitational pull, just like the pull the moon has on the earth, and the gas in your fuel tank would ebb and flow with the tides of that pull, just like the ocean. But you could happily coexist with your black hole moon for about as long as you wanted.

It's only if you drove in closer and crossed what's called the "event horizon" that you would be inexorably pulled into the gravitational space-time distortion that leads to the singularity, which is the end of the end of the end.

So what's underneath that nothingness? Obviously: weirdness. One theory is that, since a black hole is all of the matter left over when a star exploded, or two stars collided, it's possible that all the matter is compressed into a Planck star ("Planck" is the smallest possible size in physics). When it can compress no further, it would explode, making black holes temporary objects that would have lifespans of only trillions of years.

Another theory is that some black holes might actually be gravastars, which are filled with dark energy, a substance that also distorts space-time and causes it to expand outward. But more and more signals picked up from real black holes by the Laser Interferometer Gravitational-Wave Observatory are casting doubt on the existence of gravastars. That's not to say there's not dark energy in black holes—some scientists believe they are the source of all dark energy, which is the energy that's believed to be driving the unexplainable and unceasing expansion of the universe.

The problem with all these theories is that black holes out in the wild are pretty wild. The idea of a singularity, a central point of infinite density, being the center of a black hole is assuming that it's just sitting there, like a boring heap. In reality, many black holes are rotating, creating a catastrophic centrifugal force. And their interiors are tragically unstable. So that single point of no return is more likely to be a ring, stretched in unpredictable ways by its own spin.

According to Einstein's theory of general relativity, if you passed through that ring of singularity, you would enter a wormhole and pop out through a white hole in a completely new part of the universe. (Naturally, a white hole is the opposite of a black hole: nothing can enter it and matter gushes out at the speed of light.)

Scientists speculate that whatever's going on inside a black hole could mimic the creation of the universe, when time and space came into existence. And that the Big Bang may have been more of a "big bounce"—that as matter was compressed into the density of a Planck length, it then exploded outward again, and will continue to do so, on and on and ON. Sheesh, we get it, universe.

Luckily, there is absolutely no way to prove any of this because the closest black hole to us is 1,566 light-years away, and the spaghettifying thing is still an issue. But in November 2022, scientists created a lab-grown black hole analog that proved one of Stephen Hawking's theories: that black holes can summon light into existence.

The lab-rat black hole showed that the event horizon at the mouth of a black hole has a warping effect that creates uneven pockets of differently moving time and spikes of energy, and it's these mismatches in energy that cause particles to come into existence from what appears to be nothing. These particles then flare and explode, and the soft glow created by them is called Hawking radiation.

If you now need to pour your brain back into your skull, here's a reassuring fact: there are no black holes anywhere near earth. And even if our sun were replaced with a black hole of the same mass, it wouldn't suck our planet in. Even better, the sun will never turn into a black hole. It's not big enough of a star for that.

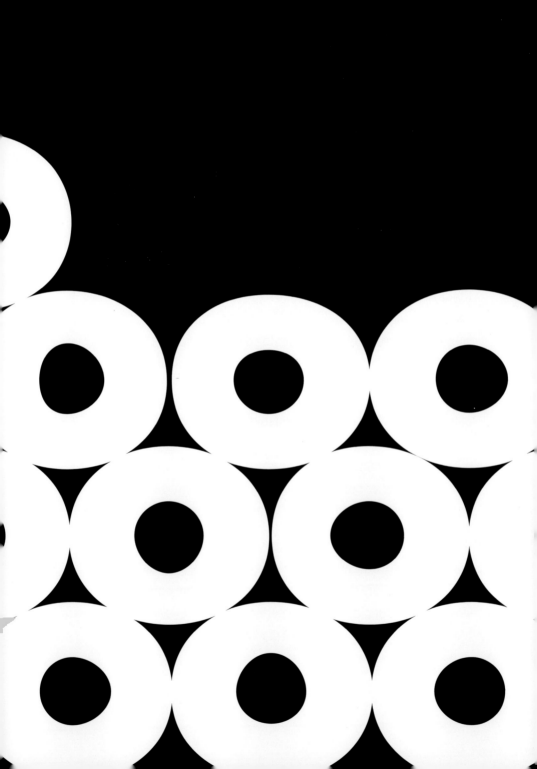

7

Sports Reports
Out of Left Field

The Fast and the Furriest: Five Fanciful Animal Competitions around the World

Racers, start your ostriches and ready your rabbits! All around the world, competitions are taking place to determine the greatest (and usually cutest) animal athletes around. Jump into these highly anticipated sporting events.

1.
Rabbit show jumping in Sweden

Known as *Kaninhoppning* in Swedish, rabbit show jumping has these domesticated fluffballs soaring over obstacles, dashing through courses, and landing right into our hearts for a perfect ten.

2.
Wiener dog races in the US

What's funnier than watching a sausage dog run? How about watching a sausage dog run while dressed in their Halloween best? This is the ingenious thinking that brought us Texas's annual wiener dog races (and chili cook-off, but that's just a bonus).

3.
Camel beauty pageants in the UAE

She is beauty; she is grace. She . . . has some spittle on her face? The Al Dhafra Festival's camel beauty pageant is one of its most highly anticipated events, and it's no wonder why. Decked out from hump to toe, the pageant's whiskered contestants are a sight to behold, and all deserve first place in our hearts.

4.
Ostrich races in South Africa

Another event for long-necked companions, ostrich races take place every day in the South African town of Oudtshoorn. The locale is known for its ostrich farms and skilled ostrich-riding jockeys, who reach speeds of forty miles per hour while racing these flightless sprinters.

5.
Elephant soccer in Nepal

Nepalese mahouts (elephant handlers) work with their pachyderm partners and compete in the Chitwan Elephant Festival's elephant soccer match every December. Just like a scene from *Ratatouille*, the tiny driver leads their steed around the soccer field while the elephant nudges the ball into the goal, making the crowd go wild!

Why Baseball
Is Batting 1000 from
America to Japan

Born in Cooperstown, New York, in 1839, baseball has long held the title of "America's Pastime Sport," but there is one island nation that rivals America's love of the game. Halfway across the world, Japan has been playing baseball for almost as long and also considers it the country's national sport. Baseball is consistently the most attended team sporting event in Japan, and the population's passion for it has produced some of the greatest players of all time, like Masahiro Tanaka and Shohei Ohtani. Japan has even beaten the US at its own game (literally) with a 3–2 win against America in the 2023 World Baseball Classic, a win that also secured the team the tournament trophy.

But how did baseball find itself so far from home in the first place? While there's a popular misconception that the sport was introduced to Japan during American occupation after WWII, it actually made landfall much earlier in 1872 by way of an American professor. Professor Horace Wilson was originally brought to postwar Japan by the US government to aid in modernizing the Japanese education system. He then continued to work in the country as an English professor at Tokyo's Kaisei Academy, which is where he taught students how to play baseball. Long story shortstop, the game was a home run. The first organized team of adult players was formed soon after in 1878, and the earliest professional competitions got going in the 1920s. And the rest is baseball history.

Obscure Baseball Facts
That Will Throw You a Curveball

Baseballs used in Major League games are held together with 108 double stitches, which gives the pitcher a better grip and improves the spin of the ball midair.

The game was an official Olympic sport until it was dropped in 2008. But it made one more appearance in the 2020 summer games, which were hosted in, you guessed it, Japan.

Left-handed people are pretty rare, but left-handed MLB catchers are even rarer. In fact, most left-handed players aren't allowed to play the catcher position, which is why there hasn't been one since 1989.

Flat-Ironing the Competition

Best described in the words of the Extreme Ironing Bureau (a legit organization, we swear), extreme ironing is "the latest danger sport that combines the thrills of an extreme outdoor activity with the satisfaction of a well-pressed shirt." Not sold on the idea yet? We totally understand, but our collective confusion hasn't stopped ironing enthusiasts from scrambling up summits in pursuit of peak athleticism and perfectly pressed trousers since the sport's invention in 1997.

The brainchild of Englishman Phil Shaw, extreme ironing was conceived out of boredom. Shaw had a simple problem (ironing his clothes was incredibly boring), so his solution was making a simple change of scenery. First, he ironed in his backyard. Then, he took things further. Before long, he found himself straightening by the sea, flattening with a fern, and pleating on a pinnacle. It didn't take long for people to catch wind of his laundry routine of choice, and the first Extreme Ironing World Championships took place in 2002 with twelve teams of passionate "ironists" vying for the fastest completion time and the crispest linens. Sadly, this was the first and final championship. However, many other amazing feats have continued to be accomplished in the name of the sport, including Everest climbers pressing the Union Jack at the mountain's peak, eighty-six divers simultaneously ironing while underwater, and a few particularly daring attempts on horseback.

Why Pickleball Became a Big Dill

Does it seem like everyone you know is now playing pickleball? Well, you're going to have to dill with it—this weirdly named sport is taking over the world. While there has been a surge in popularity since the pandemic, the game was actually invented in 1965. Three dads came up with it while trying to keep their bored families amused on a summer day in Bainbridge Island, Washington. Joel Pritchard, Barney McCallum, and Bill Bell had a badminton net but not enough rackets. Because they're dads, and therefore a little goofy, they grabbed some ping-pong paddles and a plastic whiffle ball instead.

The rules evolved as more families played the game, with the name coming from Joel's wife, Joan, who was a rower. "To hear my mother tell it, they sort of threw the leftover non-starter oarsmen into these particular pickle boats," said her son, Frank. "She thought pickleball sort of threw bits of other games into the mix (badminton, table tennis) and decided that 'Pickle Ball' was an appropriate name." (Mark this as the first time in history someone decided the appropriate thing to do was throw in the word "pickle.")

After a few years, the first court was built in Joel's friend's backyard. A few years after that, the first tournament was hosted, drawing a ton of tennis players (they admit that pickleball is where they go to die). By 1972, pickleball was an official sport. One of players in the first tournament was Steve Paranto, an engineer at Boeing who devised a lighter replacement for the heavy wooden paddles. After producing one thousand of the fiberglass paddles, he sold the company. Which was not his best financial move—the global pickleball paddle market reached $158.4 million in 2022. Sorry, Steve.

The sport has grown in popularity over the years, including increasing 159 percent in the years after the pandemic. This growth is in part because it is so darn easy to learn. The ball moves at one-third of the speed of a tennis ball, so most people can hit it. The oldest registered player is ninety-four and the youngest is four. With its small court size, it has become a staple in school gym classes and among the retired set, with more than 4.8 million "picklers" estimated in the United States and 8.9 million worldwide.

As one of America's fastest-growing sports, pickleball now has two national tournaments with corporate sponsors. It also has its own lingo, including terms such as "dink" for a drop shot; a "falafel," which is a shot so slow it doesn't make it over the net; and a "flapjack," which is a ball that must bounce before it can be hit. But in order to become an Olympic sport, it needs competitive players in seventy-five countries, a number the International Federation of Pickleball is actually close to reaching.

And with fame also comes ego . . . pickleball now has its own superstars. The highest-earning professional pickler to date is Ben Johns, considered by some to be the best of all time ("all time" being a whole fifty-eight years). He has dominated the three divisions for years, including a 108-game winning streak in singles. Before he came to the sport, he played both tennis and table tennis, so he was good at racket sports. But he credits a bookshelf for helping him in pickleball.

"Growing up, I had a bookcase on the left side of the table in our basement," Johns said in an interview, "and usually in table tennis you run around your backhand and hit your forehand loop. I couldn't, because of the shelf. So I ended up hitting a lot of backhands from every part of the court, which has helped me in pickleball." The sport runs in the family, as he often plays doubles with his brother, Collin, and is interviewed by his sister, Hannah, a sideline reporter.

Johns says that one of the things that he loves about the sport is that it's still evolving. "Everyone is adding new shots and strategies all the time—meaning that nobody really knows the 'correct' things to do.... That's what makes it a lot of fun." Who knows, maybe your signature dink will become the "alley-oop" of pickleball!

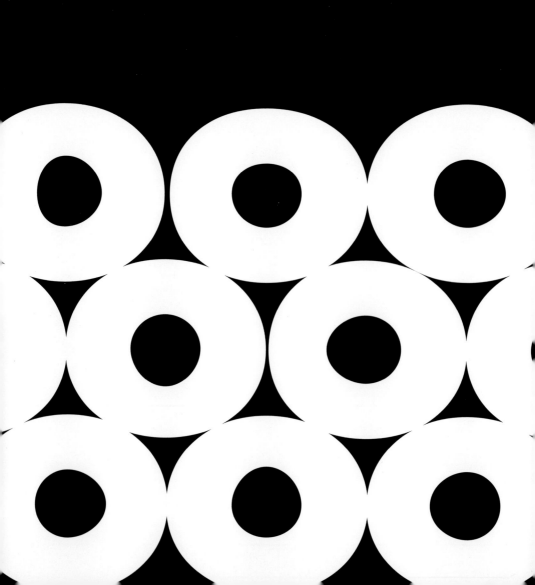

8

Travel Notes to Roam This Weird World

The Principality of Sealand: The World's Smallest Micronation

If you ever find yourself vacationing on the chilly shore of Suffolk, England, you may spy something strange in the water. Not the Loch Ness Monster on its own holiday—the mysterious smudge you would spot in the distance is the Principality of Sealand, which is one of the roughly 140 micronations dotted around the world. A micronation is any political entity that claims to be an independent nation but isn't legally acknowledged by an officially recognized sovereign state, and, yes, you could technically make one yourself.

Coming in at just over 43,000 square feet (that's smaller than a standard football field, which is 57,600 square feet!), Sealand claims to be the tiniest micronation on Earth. But how did this former British sea fort become the international outlaw that it is today? The principality's beginnings go back to World War II when the Royal Navy began setting up strategic outposts in the UK's surrounding waters. Originally built in 1942 and named HM Fort Roughs, the elevated platform that would become Sealand was eventually abandoned to decay in the international waters by 1956 and would stay that way until it was occupied by a former British Army major a decade later.

After serving the British Armed Forces, Major Paddy Roy Bates turned his attention to a different rebel passion of his: pirate radio. He never got around to starting up his broadcast, but he did find the inspiration to declare Fort Roughs an independent nation, rename it the Principality of Sealand, and dub himself prince. Since its founding, the micronation has achieved a peak population of fifty people, issued its own currency and postage stamps, founded the Sealand National Football Association, and, most importantly, evaded significant territorial disputes with the UK. The micronation has also been able to generate money as an offshore internet hosting facility and by selling aristocratic titles, so you can also be a lord or lady of this distinguished locale.

Three More Little Facts about Micronations

1. Australia is home to more than a dozen micronations, making it the micronation macrocapital of the world.

2. The Micronational Football Association, or MFA, is the biggest soccer organization for micronations and has members from thirteen different "countries."

3. Although difficult to track exactly, there are an estimated four hundred micronations worldwide.

Off-Road and Offbeat: Five Marvelously Mystifying Roadside Attractions

According to the Bureau of Serious Statistics (or BSS), "Are we there yet?" is the first symptom to appear in over 99.99 percent of cases of Low-Roadtrip-Vibes (LRV) syndrome. This chronic disease devastates millions of travelers worldwide every year and has been the beginning of the end for countless road-weary vacationers. Thankfully, the research institute of Health Advisors for Happy Adventurers (or HAHA) have proposed a cure: weird roadside attractions. From gargantuan pineapples to the Umbrella Cover Museum, these are four tourist attractions from around the globe that will cure even the most dire cases of LRV.

1.
An enormous pineapple

Not living in a pineapple under the sea, the pineapple people in the Eastern Cape Province of South Africa have been growing the prickly fruit since 1865 (that's over 150 years!). For this area, pineapple isn't just a food but a lifestyle, and what better way to celebrate that than constructing a 55-foot-tall fiberglass pineapple with a 360-degree view? That's right, nothing.

2.
The "only" for a reason

Proud to be home to "The World's Only Corn Palace," Mitchell, South Dakota, is a small town off of Route 90 with a big appreciation for corn. The Corn Palace is decorated with murals made from twelve different shades of corn. Even better, the building is redecorated every year, so it's a spot that you'll *definitely* want to revisit.

3.
A topsy-turvy townhouse

Just south of Shanghai, the Chinese Folk Painting Village located in Fengjing Ancient Town built one house that turned things in the village on its head—literally! From the foundation to the furniture, this upside-down house isn't raising the roof, but it will have you dancing on the ceiling.

4.
So weird it's good

The Umbrella Cover Museum in Maine exclusively displays one item: the flimsy covers that come with umbrellas. The museum's founder, Nancy 3. Hoffman (yes, her middle initial is a number), says that she was inspired to open the exhibit after stealing the cover off an umbrella from a dollar store. Since this act of kleptomania, the collection has grown to include different umbrella covers from all over the world, winning this attraction the final slot on our list.

Two Words: POOPOOPAPER Park

Known for its white sand beaches, exotic wildlife, and ornate architecture set in lush landscapes, Thailand attracts millions of tourists every year. With so much foot traffic, protections are in place to conserve the country's many natural wonders. But some conservation efforts are definitely more "unique" (and giggle-inducing) than others.

Located in the northern city of Chiang Mai, Elephant POOPOOPAPER Park (the capitalization is completely accurate, we swear) is an outdoor museum dedicated to teaching visitors about sustainability and the process of making paper from—you guessed it—elephant poop! Run by the company POOPOOPAPER (again, this is an *actual* name), the park was created to highlight Chiang Mai's long history of paper making and to let people get down and dirty with the company's own way of making recycled paper. Starting with a pile of dry droppings, tourists are encouraged to smell and even *touch* the pre-paper poop. Guides then walk visitors through the process of cleaning the raw material, extracting fibers, boiling paste, and drying the poo-parchment on screens under the sun, which will then become eco-friendly paper products, like stationery, sketchbooks, and more! So, would this be our number one tourist destination if we were visiting Thailand? Probably not, but it would be our number two!

Dubai Has Literal Desert Islands

If hours of window-shopping on Zillow have taught us anything, it's that 1) hardwood floors are a must, and 2) property value is all about location, location, location. But what if we could get around the location problem by making our own tropical paradise? Well, this was (probably) the exact thinking of Dubai's leaders when they decided to build their own islands off the coast of the city *from scratch*.

Beginning in 2001, government officials and local real estate developers decided to break new ground by proposing a megaproject that would create three palmed-shaped islands. The man-made collection of archipelagos was creatively declared "the Palm Islands" and were individually called Palm Jumeirah, Palm Jebel Ali, and Deira Islands (–5 points for no naming consistency). To construct one island, land developers drew up three billion cubic feet of sand from Dubai's shallow seafloor and used GPS coordinates to painstakingly mold the sand into a palm tree with seventeen palms. But the work didn't stop there. Next, roughly seven million tons of rock were arranged around the frond to make a seven-mile long crescent around the newly minted landmass.

So, what was the point of all this trouble? To increase the coastline and pivot the United Arab Emirates' economy away from just oil to another high-profit market: luxury tourism! Lined with high-end resorts and shopping malls for days, this project was designed to be a shopaholic's dream come true. While this was the goal, the islands' ultimate legacy was a little less light-hearted because, believe it or not, just because

something is plant-shaped doesn't make it good for the environment. As it turns out, the islands' construction stirred up a lot of sediment and even more criticism from environmentalists, which was harsh enough to pause further expansion. So, if the Palm Islands have taught us anything, it's that location might not be everything.

Inside Nishiyama Onsen Keiunkan, the World's Oldest Hotel

Nestled deep in the mountains of Japan's Yamanashi prefecture, Nishiyama Onsen Keiunkan promises relaxing hot springs and a portal to a bygone era just east of the bustling metropolis of Tokyo. The traditional Japanese inn, or *ryokan*, has preserved a lot of its original aesthetic and operations management style from when it was opened in 705 CE. Yes, you read that date correctly. This hotel was opened before Kyoto (one of Japan's former capital cities) was founded in 794 and before Tokyo was officially founded in 1889. Basically, this place is *old* old.

The inn was established during Japan's Keiun era and reflected in the name "Keiunkan." Legend has it that its founder, Fujiwara Mahito, was wandering the area when he came across a beautiful hot spring. Hot springs are abundant across the country, and business-savvy people often opened up onsen-style baths and inns for customers looking for a relaxing staycation. It goes without saying that Nishiyama Onsen Keiunkan's scenic views made this location an obvious "yes."

For the low, low price of 52,000 yen (or roughly $350), you can still experience the historic inn of shoguns and emperors. Upon your arrival, you will be greeted by picturesque mountain vistas, handwritten calligraphy, and staff dressed in traditional kimono. Most rooms have one living room and two sitting rooms with tatami mat floors. The bedding is hidden away until nighttime when the staff sets it out. And of course, visitors can enjoy indoor or outdoor baths after their five-course meal of local delicacies. Now this is what we mean by vacationing!

Things You Probably Didn't Know
about Japanese Onsens

The naturally heated water that feeds into an onsen can reach boiling temperatures, but a more typical temperature is around 40 degrees Celsius or 104 degrees Fahrenheit. Some places used these super-hot waters to cook food, like boiled eggs!

Dogo Onsen is another one of the oldest hot springs in Japan, and descriptions of the spring have appeared in ancient texts written over three thousand years ago.

The government has very strict requirements for what counts as an onsen, like having to have water with at least one of nineteen specific minerals and having a natural temperature of least 25 degrees Celsius or 77 degrees Fahrenheit.

Class Action Park, the World's Most Dangerous Water Park

If you grew up in the early '80s in New Jersey or New York, you couldn't escape the ads for Action Park. Kids lucky enough to go told shocking stories of underage drinking and near-death experiences. Newspapers regularly ran articles about the horrific injuries and ongoing lawsuits. This, of course, made kids want to go even more. A visit to Action Park felt like a rite of passage—one that not everyone survived.

When the park opened in 1978, it was one of the first to have water rides. Some of the attractions were so innovative that it was questionable whether they had ever been tested. A knee-knocking favorite was the Tidal Wave Pool, which was often packed with hundreds of people. For twenty minutes at a time, waves as high as three feet rose above the twelve-foot-deep water, crashing down over and over again. If you weren't a strong swimmer, you would soon find yourself fighting the tall waves, your short, foolish life flashing before your eyes.

With people screaming and scrambling as the waves hit, it was hard for lifeguards to tell who was having fun and who was having trouble staying afloat. On busy weekends, they had to pull hundreds of people out of the pool, adding "saved from a watery grave" to the park's roster of attractions. But they couldn't save everyone. In 1982, the first person drowned. Two years later, a second died. In 1987, a third man drowned. Yet, the ride—which employees nicknamed "Grave Pool"—stayed open.

Action Park's founder, Gene Mulvihill, believed that visitors should set their own limits and create their own experiences. That's why the park's slogan was "Where *you* are in the center of the action." His rides allowed visitors to determine how fast or high or far they went—sort of like running your own roller coaster while you were riding it.

Mulvihill, who was either an innovator or a mad scientist, often dreamed up rides and then paid his employees to try them out. If they didn't get too injured, he'd open them to the public. The park didn't break any regulations because the rides were often so new there weren't any rules yet to break. His son Andy later said, "My father, if he could find a guy with a crazy idea for a ride, he'd hire the guy, even if he never built it before."

The Cannonball Loop was one such invention—it was a waterslide with a 360-degree turn in the middle. In theory, a rider would plummet down a steep hill in a rush of water, hit the loop fast, and then splash out of the other end into a shallow pool. But in practice, people's faces hit the top of the loop so hard they were losing teeth and breaking noses. This is one of the rare rides that actually closed quickly at Action Park, although Mulvihill kept tinkering and periodically reopening it to allow a few more people to possibly have their teeth knocked out.

Other treacherous rides stayed open for decades, like the Alpine Slide, a series of wheeled plastic sleds that rode on a concrete track straight down the side of a steep mountain. Each sled had a brake so you could control your speed . . . when the brakes worked. Of course, you didn't find out if they did or not until you were already hurtling down the track.

The only rule on the Alpine Slide was to keep your arms inside the sled. Otherwise, it was a *Mad Max* free-for-all. When their brakes failed, riders might crash into the sled in front of them. Or a sled might take a turn too fast and jump the track. Or a teenage speed demon would ram a slower rider in their way.

As there was no safety harness or padding, if riders fell off the sled, the concrete would provide a nice, cushy landing. But the Alpine Slide remained incredibly popular, even though riders fell off daily and at least twenty-six head injuries and fourteen broken bones were reported to the state. In 1980, a nineteen-year-old's sled jumped the

tracks, causing him to hit his head on a rock and die. But the park's defense was that it was the rock that killed the teen, not the ride, so of course they were blameless. The ride stayed open.

Another questionable attraction at the park was the gladiator challenge, where employees would beat the tar out of visitors. This was all done in the guise of a "joust." One time a man lost so badly he came back with his friends for revenge. The confrontation escalated into a huge rumble where both employees and visitors were pulling bricks out of the walkway to throw at each other. (Remember, this was in New Jersey.)

The hazardous rides combined with the park's many beer stands meant there were injuries every single day—so many that Mulvihill bought the park its own ambulance. But the very real and present danger did not stop the crowds from coming. By 1986, the park was packed every weekend, with half-drunk teenage workers running rides with little thought to safety protocols. That wild summer 330 injuries were reported to the state, with as many as ten times that not officially recorded. Many people just took their bleeding limbs to the park's first aid shed. Once their wounds were sprayed with the stinging combination of rubbing alcohol and iodine, they were sent on their way to their next near-death experience.

Much of this perilous amusement was made possible by Action Park's ingenious legal strategy. A team of lawyers mounted a strong defense against every claim, with the ace up their sleeve being a series of signs posted throughout the park with the warning to visitors to "participate at your own risk." But the park still paid out hefty settlements. In 1996, the lawsuits got to be too much and a bankruptcy closed the park for good. Sadly, daredevil kids and irresponsible parents were left to risk life and limb in their own backyards.

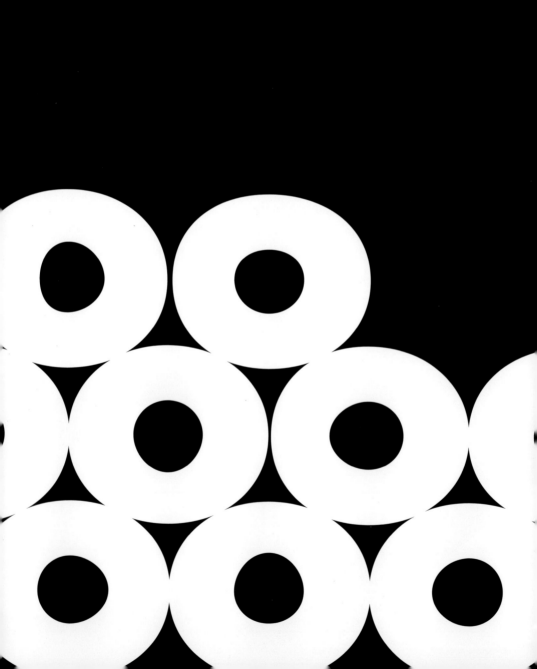

9

Crimes & Mysteries
Stranger Than
Fan Fiction

Crime Nor Reason: Six Bizarre Ways to Break the Law

Everyone strives to be a law-abiding citizen (except for the occasional jaywalking offense), but some of us might be hardened criminals and not even realize it. This is because of a few oddly specific rules around the world that set up some unexpected run-ins with the law. So, keep reading to stay in the know and out of the slammer.

1.

In Scotland you are legally obligated to let anyone use your toilet if they ask. In other news, proposed legislation mandating every restroom must own a copy of *The Modern Bathroom Reader* has (sadly) not been reviewed by the Scottish Parliament ... yet.

2.

Pop quiz: In which US state is it illegal to carry an ice cream cone in your back pocket? If you guessed Kentucky, you're correct! If you said Georgia, then you're also correct but only on Sundays (pocket-ice-cream is perfectly legal any other day of the week, *whew*).

3.

Swiss law dictates that all guinea pig owners must have at least two guinea pigs at a time. This is because these precious furballs are social creatures and need a companion to be happy, a fact too adorable not to legislate.

4.

Forgetting your wife's birthday in Samoa can land you up to five years in prison. We nominate this law to win the award for "Most Creative Excuse to Party."

5.

It is illegal to fart in public after 6:00 p.m. in Florida by penalty of law. Who knew people took public noise ordinances so seriously?

6.

In the Philippines you can be fined or imprisoned for up to thirty days (or both!) for the offense of "unjust vexation." In other words, it's illegal to be annoying.

Yummy, Yummy, Yummy, We've Got Mummies in Our Tummies

When we hear "cannibalism," our minds probably imagine savage practices of ancient times or last-resort decisions in desperate situations. After all, the Donner Party proved that nothing gets someone "lookin' like a snack" more than a long and hungry winter.

But would you believe us if we told you that cannibalism happened regularly in Europe and that it was going on all the way into the seventeenth century? Well, to readers who are easily nauseated, look away, because it is absolutely true. The Europeans' long and unhealthy obsession with Egyptian mummies wasn't satisfied by just breaking into ancient, sacred tombs and robbing them of both their earthly possessions and their human remains; they also felt the need *to eat the remains.* From kings to commoners, people were convinced that you could cure a plethora of illnesses taking a pinch of powdered mummy, called "mumia" (yes, this was an actual product, we swear!).

Although mummy-medicine-mania peaked in the seventeenth century, it tapped into a much older homeopathic belief that "like cured like." So, if you had a headache, you should take a tincture mixed with ground-up skull. Or you might be told to drink blood to fix a blood disease. So there was technically some method to the madness, we guess? Besides this, some people thought that these cannibal concoctions carried remnants of the deceased person's spirit, which would strengthen the patient's own vitality. Luckily, by the nineteenth century everyone agreed that eating people was a no-good, very bad thing to do. By this time, the Victorians were happy just to host mummy unwrapping parties, which also wasn't great but was definitely a shambling step in the right direction.

Was Amelia Earhart
Eaten by Giant Crabs?

If you don't have nightmares about crabs, well…welcome to a new chapter in your life. Meet the coconut crab, which lives in the Pacific and Indian Oceans. This hellspawn with claws can weigh nine pounds, grow as wide as three feet across, and live as long as one hundred years. Its pincers are strong enough to crack coconuts, which make up the majority of its diet. If you've ever tried to open a coconut, you know it's not easy breezy island fun, much less with one hand (um, claw).

But a crab doesn't grow to those terrifying proportions without being willing to eat anything in its path. With their great sense of smell, these land crabs sniff out prey, both living and dead. And to haunt your dreams, they typically wait until night to attack, and they eat everything from rats to seabird chicks to kittens to other coconut crabs. Scientists have even witnessed them demolish a small pig. In a pinch, they'll even eat their own exoskeletons after they molt. (This would be like eating your own flaked off skin, in case you needed a visual.)

Now what do coconut crabs have to do with famed aviator Amelia Earhart? Well, they may have been the last creatures to see her alive. When Earhart turned forty, she decided she was ready to be the first woman to fly around the world. At the time she had broken multiple flight records, so she knew the trip was dangerous. "I want to do it because I want to do it," she wrote.

Earhart and her navigator, Fred Noonan, squeezed into the small plane and took off from Oakland, California, on May 20, 1937. Most of the space was taken up for gas to fuel their long flight. They hopscotched

from airfield
to airfield,
eventually taking
off from Lae, New
Guinea, on July 2.
Earhart made radio
contact with a coast guard
cutter anchored off their next
destination of Howland Island.
But they never reached that tiny speck
halfway between Australia and Hawaii,
disappearing somewhere in the Pacific.

The navy launched a huge and expensive search, including following up on the multiple distress calls they'd received. But the area where the plane could potentially be was the size of Texas and located in the middle of nowhere. After ten days, they called off the search and concluded that the plane was lost somewhere in the Pacific Ocean.

Some came to believe that Earhart and Noonan crash-landed near the tiny island of Nikumaroro, which is about four hundred miles from Howland Island. A flyover search of the 4.7-mile-long island showed signs of habitation, but no one waved them down and the rescue team didn't land to investigate. In a photo of the island taken months after Earhart disappeared, there is a shadow in the water near the island that was later thought to be the landing gear of their plane. So in 2019, Dr. Robert Ballard, the man known for finding the wreck of the *Titanic*, led a two-week, multimillion-dollar investigation to find the plane, which some believe fell into the deep chasms that surround the island.

155

The expensive venture was a long shot—more than eighty years had passed—and they not surprisingly found bupkis.

Even so, other evidence convinced experts that Earhart and Noonan had landed on the reef surrounding Nikumaroro. In 1940, in a hard-to-reach part of the uninhabited island, a British officer found evidence of a campfire, animal bones, a box that had once contained a sextant similar to the one Noonan used, and pieces of a man's shoe and a woman's shoe. Human bones were also found. A scientist who examined them at the time initially thought they belonged to a man. But then the bones somehow disappeared, just like Earhart. In 2022, scientists ran the information recorded in 1940 about the bones through forensic software. It was a 99 percent match with Earhart. But some researchers remain understandably skeptical, as the conclusion is drawn from measurements taken decades ago on bones that no one can now find.

So, what happened to Earhart? While no one ever lived on Nikumaroro, it *was* inhabited by giant coconut crabs. Some believe the reason Earhart was never found was that her body was devoured by the scavengers. And that might have suited her just fine. Before her final trip, Earhart told a reporter, "As far as I know I've only got one obsession—a small and probably typically feminine horror of growing old—so I won't feel completely cheated if I fail to come back."

A Con Man So Smooth He Sold the Eiffel Tower

In 1925, Victor Lustig pulled off one of the greatest cons in history. Posing as a government official in Paris, Lustig convinced scrap metal dealers that the seven-thousand-ton Eiffel Tower had structural problems. Originally built for the World's Fair, he claimed the now-rusting tower had to be torn down and sold for scrap. Even better, he convinced the dealers that, because the tower was so beloved, they had to keep it on the hush-hush that they were bidding on the job. (Genius.)

Lustig then went on to "sell" the rights to the highest bidder, quickly absconding with the loot. The scrap dealer was so embarrassed at being conned that he didn't report the crime, and it only came to light when Lustig pushed his luck and tried to sell it a *second* time. (Lesson: Never run the same con twice, kids.) He fled France before being arrested but not before authorities began to wonder, "Who was this man?"

Raised in poverty in Austria-Hungary, he changed his name, somehow made himself a count, became fluent in five languages, and acquired more than forty-seven aliases, a trunk of disguises, and dozens of passports. His cons included every card game and swindle imaginable, which he plied on the wealthy sailing from Europe to America, where he finally settled in 1920.

Lustig soon became known to police forces in all the major cities, recognizable for a large scar on his cheek given to him by a romantic rival in his younger days. He was not a violent man—he'd rather use his wits than a gun. One of his most notorious cons was called the Rumanian money box, a device that supposedly used radium to

reproduce money. He claimed each bill took six hours to produce. By having his customers load two real $100 bills into the box, it gave Lustig twelve hours to get away after selling a box. He was so good that he convinced a Texas sheriff to buy one for thousands of dollars. When the sheriff later tracked him down, Lustig convinced him that he was just using the box wrong.

The charming Lustig not only conned the law but also duped criminals, including legendary crime boss Al Capone. He convinced the mobster to invest $50,000 in a con. Weeks passed and Lustig returned the money, saying the job had fallen through. Capone believed he could now trust the con man, and when Lustig asked Capone to give him the $5,000 he had lost on the job, the crime boss happily forked over the money. For absolutely nothing.

As confusing as his cons could be, Lustig had rules he lived by, which included "Be a patient listener" and "Never look bored." He believed that people love to hear themselves talk, and that was how a mark would eventually reveal the information needed. He also prided himself on being a gentleman, and he believed a con man should "Never be untidy" and "Never get drunk." He was so smooth and smart that even though he was arrested thirty-seven times, he was never convicted. An agent at the time described the wanted criminal as "elusive as cigarette smoke and as charming as a young girl's dream."

What finally put Lustig in the crosshairs of the Secret Service was counterfeiting. He had teamed up with a talented forger to make fake $100 bills. The money was so well done that it passed scrutiny by bank tellers. In 1935, after a lengthy pursuit, Lustig was caught with a key to a locker that contained $51,000 in fake bills and the plates from which they were printed. There was no talking his way out of these charges.

This con sent Lustig to the escape-proof Federal House of Detention in New York . . . from which he quickly escaped. Using a rope made out of sheets, he lowered himself out of the prison window. He did it in full view of dozens of witnesses, pretending that he was washing the windows as he made his way down to the ground, where he promptly took off on foot.

Lustig was caught in Pittsburgh a few weeks later. The jailbreak caused him to be sentenced to twenty years in the inescapable Alcatraz prison, where, after more than one thousand medical complaints, Lustig died of pneumonia in 1947. It turns out no one, not even the world's greatest con man, can cheat death.

How a Socialite's Murders in Miniature Changed Forensics Forever

Frances Glessner Lee knew she was lucky to be born in 1878 to rich parents. She once wrote, "I didn't do a lick of work to deserve what I have. Therefore, I feel I have been left an obligation to do something that will benefit everybody." In 1936, she gave $250,000 of the money she inherited from her family's agricultural machine fortune to Harvard to help create the Department of Legal Medicine. It was one of the first places in the country to research the causes of unexplained death.

Lee became interested in the topic through a family friend, George Burgess Magrath, who studied with her brother at Harvard. She grew up being homeschooled and her parents thought college would be wasted on Lee, so she became a socialite and a wife. She married at twenty, had three children, then got a divorce, a rare thing for a woman to do at the time. When her children were grown, she reignited her passion for forensics. Learning about crime scenes might seem like an odd hobby for a Gilded Age heiress, but Lee was fascinated. She came to understand the importance of looking at the complete scene to find the clues.

After endowing the department, Lee created the Harvard Seminars in Homicide Investigation, where she invited experts to teach and learn about the art of crime scene detections. Twenty-five to thirty policemen would spend a week learning new ways to identify a victim, interrogate a witness, determine the time of death, and get to know others in their field. "My whole object," Lee wrote, "has been to improve the administration of justice, to standardize the methods, to sharpen the existing tools as well as supply new tools, and to make it easier for the law enforcement officers to 'do a good job' and to give the public 'a square deal.'"

Through these conversations and seminars, Lee conceived of the Nutshell Studies. The name came from a police adage: "As the investigator, you must bear in mind that there is a two-fold responsibility—to clear the innocent as well as expose the guilty. Seek only the facts—find the truth in a nutshell."

In 1943, Lee used her skills learned as a lady in high society, including painting, sewing, and making miniatures, to begin building mind-numbingly detailed dioramas of crime scenes in actual cases. Her goal was to have them be used as police training tools. These miniature, dollhouse-like rooms showed the dead, who ranged from prostitutes to victims of domestic violence, exactly how they were found. Each study included background information on the case along with clues for investigating the crime.

The spaces were scaled at one foot to one inch and included any details important to the case, such as windows that opened, rolling pins that rolled, and working lights. To make sure that the corpses and blood splatters were exactly what an investigator would find, she visited crime scenes and attended autopsies. "An effort has been made to illustrate not only the death that occurred but the social and financial status of those involved, as well as their frame of mind at the time the death took place," she wrote. Lee often featured victims that were poor or living on the fringes of society, so investigators would learn to overcome their unconscious biases and pursue the case with vigor.

Lee painstakingly finished around three nutshells a year for a total of twenty, each costing more than $3,000 to create. In a letter to the dean, she wrote, "I found myself constantly tempted to add more clues and details and am afraid I may get them 'gadgety' in the process. I hope you will watch over this and stop me when I go too far."

One study, known as the Kitchen, shows a woman lying dead on the floor. In the accompanying statement, the woman's husband, Fred Barnes, told police that he had left his wife to go into town. When he returned, the doors to the house were locked. When his wife didn't answer the knock, he looked in the kitchen window to find her lying there. He then called the police.

Investigators were tasked with determining whether her death was due to natural causes, accident, suicide, or homicide. Tucked into the nutshell were clues, such as fingerprints and an unlocked window, that pointed to how Fred had murdered his wife. "A person studying these models can learn more about circumstantial evidence in an hour than he could learn in months of abstract study," said Erle Stanley Gardner, the writer who created the *Perry Mason* mysteries and Mrs. Lee's close friend.

These studies helped investigators learn how to search a room, gather evidence, and analyze a crime scene. At seminars, police trainees were given witness statements, a flashlight, and a magnifying glass to review the dioramas. At the end of ninety minutes they had to present their conclusions and determine the cause of death. Lee wrote that her goal in working in this area was not just to teach technical skills but to instill in students the "unremitting quest for facts; it is a constant and continuous search for truth in the interests of science and justice, to expose the guilty, to clear the innocent."

Lee also traveled around the country, giving talks about the importance of science-based death investigations. She reached out to influential doctors, elected officials, and the head of the FBI and educated the public through exhibits at the 1933–34 Chicago World's Fair.

For her lifelong work in forensic science, Lee was made a police captain in New Hampshire, the first woman in the United States to reach that rank and the first woman invited into the International Association for Chiefs of Police. She was considered to be one of the world's most astute criminologists during her tenure there. The nutshells, which were used by police forces for decades past Lee's death in 1962, are currently with the Baltimore Medical Examiner's office and are occasionally on exhibit for curious amateur sleuths to peruse.

The Modern Bathroom Reader

Andrews McMeel Publishing
a division of Andrews McMeel Universal
1130 Walnut Street, Kansas City, Missouri 64106

www.andrewsmcmeel.com

24 25 26 27 28 SDB 10 9 8 7 6 5 4 3 2 1

ISBN: 978-1-5248-9223-4

Library of Congress Control Number: 2024943653

Editor: Marya Pasciuto and Amanda Meadows
Art Director: Holly Swayne
Production Editor: David Shaw
Production Manager: Tamara Haus

ATTENTION: SCHOOLS AND BUSINESSES
Andrews McMeel books are available at quantity discounts with bulk purchase
for educational, business, or sales promotional use. For information,
please e-mail the Andrews McMeel Publishing Special Sales Department:
sales@amuniversal.com.

FSC
www.fsc.org
MIX
Paper | Supporting
responsible forestry
FSC® C144853